Envision Your Best Life And Live It:

12 Mistakes for Young Adults to Avoid When
Manifesting
& 12 Be-Do-Have Steps to Overcome Challenges that
Will Unleash the Power of Your Imagination

Alexandria Patterson

DISCLAIMER

Table of Contents

DEDICATION

For my son, Maxwell

QUOTES

"Imagining Creates Reality"

-Neville Goddard

"Imagination is more important than knowledge."

-Albert Einstein

"It's time to start living the life you've imagined."

-Henry James

"By faith, we understand that the worlds were framed by the word of God so that the things which are seen were not made of things which are visible."

-Hebrews 11:3 (New King James Version)

INTRODUCTION

A Brief Story of My Early Beginnings into Manifesting

Growing up, I often found myself alone, left behind while my younger sibling and cousins went away for summers with their father's side of the family. I was the oldest grandchild of five, and an overprotected child, but my solitude became a canvas for creativity. I spent hours singing and dancing in front of the mirror, writing imaginary stories, and imitating characters from movies I watched over and over again. I learned early on that my imagination was a powerful tool, one that helped me create my own world when I felt isolated from the one around me.

When I was in middle school, I lived in a gang-infested neighborhood in Watts, California, for three years. It was a time of uncertainty and fear, but I found comfort and inspiration in the music of Lauryn Hill. One line from her song "Miseducation of Lauryn Hill" struck a chord with me: "I looked at my environment and wondered where the fire went, what happened to everything we used to be." That word, "environment," stayed with me. Even as a young girl, I realized I didn't have to accept my surroundings as they were. I could use my imagination to picture something different, something better.

I started to imagine a different environment for myself and my family—a calmer, safer place to live. At the time, I didn't have the words to articulate what I was doing, but I was intentionally using my imagination to create a vision of a better reality. A year later, we moved to a quiet street on the other side of town, off Slauson and Crenshaw. For two years, I lived there with my aunt and cousins, and the peace I had imagined became our daily experience. Even when I moved back to Watts to live with my momma, the neighborhood had become calmer, almost as if my vision had helped manifest a change.

From that point on, I began to see my imagination not as an escape, but as a powerful tool—a tool that could shape my experiences and bring about real change. I learned to intentionally use my imagination to create better scenarios, not just for myself, but for those around me.

Why This Book

I gathered my experiences together in this book to show that you have this same power. Your imagination is not just a place to retreat to; it's a source of strength and creativity that can help you overcome challenges and manifest the desires of your heart. I want to share my journey with you and show you how you can use your imagination to create the life you truly want to live. This book is a guide to help you unlock that potential, to help you envision your best life and make it your reality.

You, The Reader

By reading this book, you acknowledge your role as the creator of your own reality. This book serves as a gentle reminder of the steps you are already taking and provides new tools, techniques, and strategies to further aid you in manifesting the life you envision. You hold the power to design your existence on all planes - physical, mental, emotional, and spiritual. Embrace your vision for yourself, your household, your community, and even the world. This book aims to clarify the intentional manifestation process you are already doing every day. Understand that with an open mind, you can be more intentional and persistent in creating your desired reality. As you absorb the information, keep in mind that you are already familiar with these tools and techniques; now is the time to put them into action. Embrace the knowledge that you are the creator of your reality and anticipate the joy of applying these teachings in your life.

Who Am I?

Hi, I'm Alexandria, and my mission is to help people bring their inner visions to reality. Sometimes, figuring out how to make your vision a reality is tough, but I'm here to guide you every step of the way. Throughout the book, I share with you my experiences of creating my own reality through my imagination. Have you ever struggled to create the life you truly desire? I've been there. I understand what it's like to feel stuck in the routines of everyday life without knowing how to reach goals. It can be frustrating, and sometimes it feels like you're just going through the motions. But everything changed when I took the time to learn from others who were excelling.

I started to look into their journeys and discovered that many successful people have a formula that they follow. They also use their stories to inspire others, which I aim to do as well. I've made mistakes and learned valuable lessons along the way. It wasn't until I looked to those who had achieved true success that I began to see the steps I needed to follow. I've gathered all these insights into a book designed to help you bring your own vision to life.

The key to this journey lies in recognizing your potential and being creative in approaching your goals. It all starts with having a vision and understanding your own unique story. There's so much power in using your own narrative to shape your vision, and I'm excited to help you begin this incredible journey.

The 3 Parts: BE, DO, HAVE

This book is designed around three essential parts: BE, DO, and HAVE. Each part focuses on specific chapters that guide you through what you need to *be*, *do*, and *have* in the process of manifesting your desires.

In the **BE** section, you'll find chapters on Vision and Desire. From my personal experience, manifestation begins with embodying the very things you want to see in your life. I've learned that to achieve your vision and fulfill your desires, you first need to *become* them. When I visualized my goals and felt the reality of them in my mind's eye, I naturally began to attract what I longed for.

The **DO** section contains chapters on Imagination, the Power of Thoughts & Words, the Subconscious Mind and the 'How,' Thinking Bigger than Yourself, Principles from the Bible, Copying Others' Blueprint, and Knowing When to Pivot. Manifesting isn't just about wishing—it's about *doing* the work, which I like to call the "fun" instead of "work." The actions in this section are key to bringing your vision to life. Whether it's using your imagination or tapping into the power of your thoughts and words, the *doing* part is where things start to move.

Finally, in the **HAVE** section, you'll dive into chapters on your W.H.Y., setting a Due Date, and practicing Gratitude & Appreciation. Without this critical piece, it's easy to get sidetracked, distracted, or frustrated. This section is all about maintaining focus and commitment so that you can *have* what you've manifested with clarity and joy.

Your "Mistakes to Avoid"

In each chapter, I share the mistakes I've personally made while pursuing my desires, and I'm committed to helping you avoid making those same mistakes. Manifestation is a powerful process, but it's easy to get off track if you're not aware of the common pitfalls along the way. My goal is to offer you insight into the lessons I've learned so that you can navigate your own journey with greater ease and clarity.

For each mistake, I offer a practical solution you can apply to avoid falling into the same traps. This approach is designed to keep you focused on your vision and desires, helping you stay aligned with your goals while minimizing setbacks. By being aware of these potential mistakes early on, you'll be better prepared to move forward with clarity and confidence, making your path to manifestation more direct and fulfilling.

Your "Next Step"

At the end of each chapter, you'll find a section called "Next Step," which is specifically designed to help you put the ideas and concepts into action. This isn't just about reading or understanding the material—it's about *doing* something with it. Each "Next Step" offers a practical exercise, reflection, or action item that will encourage you to take what you've learned and apply it in a real and tangible way to your life.

As you move through the book, taking these steps is how you'll begin to actively shape your reality. These exercises are more than just tasks; they are small, deliberate actions that help you align with your vision and desires. By consistently engaging with them after each chapter, you'll be making steady progress toward realizing your dreams. This approach ensures that you're not just absorbing information but taking meaningful strides toward your goals, empowering you to manifest your desires with intention and purpose.

I am using etymonline.com to define words. King James Version for Bible Scriptures are used.

PART 1 - BE

You already have the vision and desire within you, and now it's time to bring them to life. Embody your vision and desire. The word 'Be' can be broken down to "I Am" or "exist," and in Latin, it is the perfect past tense "I Was." So, to 'Be' your vision and desire, you already 'ARE' your vision and desire.

1

Vision

What is Vision?

Before we get started on your vision of your life, let's break down the word "vision." In etymology, circa 1300, vision means 'something seen in the imagination or the supernatural.' In Latin, the word 'vision' comes from *visionem*, which is "act of seeing, sight, thing seen."

What do you see for yourself?

Living your life is about envisioning what you care to do, become, and have. What is your vision? Envision your future for yourself, your family, your community, your loved ones, and maybe even the world. Your vision should be impactful. When we admire the lives of others, we often forget that where they are now may result from their own aspirations and hard work. We overlook their struggles and the journey they had to undertake to achieve their goals. Everyone has a story, even those who are now wealthy and successful. Many of them came from humble beginnings, facing poverty and hardship. They had to use their imagination and determination to overcome their circumstances.

Vision is the starting point of all achievement. It is the map that guides you through the complex, winding paths of life. Without a vision, you might find yourself drifting aimlessly, unsure of your purpose or destination. But with a clear vision, you can navigate through the darkest of times, making decisions that align with your deepest desires and values. Think of vision as your inner compass, pointing you in the direction that aligns with your true self. It is more than just a fleeting dream or a vague wish; it is a powerful force that, when nurtured and cultivated, becomes the foundation upon which you build your life.

Vision vs. Reality: The Bridge of Action

While vision is where it all begins, it is not where it ends. A vision without action is like a seed without soil—it holds potential, but it will never grow unless it is planted, nurtured, and given the right conditions to flourish. This is where your imagination comes into play. Imagination is the bridge between vision and reality. It is the tool that allows you to see beyond your current circumstances and visualize a future where your dreams have come to life. But vision and imagination alone are not enough. They must be accompanied by dedication, resilience, and a willingness to take action.

Think of all the people who have made a significant impact on the world. From the great leaders who fought for freedom to the scientists who dared to challenge conventional thinking, to the artists who inspired generations with their creativity—what did they all have in common? They had a vision, and they were willing to do whatever it took to bring that vision to life. They didn't just imagine a better future; they believed in it so deeply that they were compelled to act on it. They faced countless obstacles, failures, and setbacks, but their vision kept them moving forward.

Crafting Your Vision: The Power of Clarity

To create a vision for your life, start by getting clear on what truly matters to you. Ask yourself: What do I want my life to look like in the next five, ten, or twenty years? What kind of person do I want to be? What impact do I want to have on the people around me? Think beyond material success. Consider your values, your passions, and your dreams. What kind of legacy do you want to leave behind?

Visualize it in vivid detail. Don't just think about what you want; see it in your mind's eye. Picture the colors, the sounds, the feelings associated with your vision. Allow yourself to dream big without limitations or fear. When you are clear about your vision, it will serve as a source of motivation, guiding your choices and actions. Every decision you make, big or small, will be influenced by your vision. When faced with challenges, you will find the strength to persevere because you know where you're headed.

Your Vision: A Catalyst for Change

Remember, your vision is not just about personal gain; it can be a catalyst for positive change. What if your vision could change not only your life but also the lives of others? What if, through your vision, you could contribute to something larger than yourself? Many people who have created impactful lives did so by thinking beyond their immediate needs. They envisioned a future where they could help others, create opportunities, or solve problems that affected their communities or even the world.

As you shape your vision, think about how it could benefit those around you. Consider how your unique talents, skills, and passions could be used to make a difference. Your vision could be the spark that ignites a movement, a new idea, or a solution to a problem that affects many.

So, what is your vision?

My Lack of Vision with Going to College

As the Bible verse Proverbs 29:18 states, "Where there is no vision, the people perish." I will help you understand the significance of having a vision and explain why lacking one can lead to sadness, despair, and defeat with my story below.

When I was in high school, I felt pressure to attend college because everyone around me was talking about it. I applied to different colleges without a clear idea of what I wanted to pursue. This lack of direction left me feeling lost. Eventually, it led to not being accepted or rejected by any of the schools I applied to. This experience left me feeling depressed and unsure of what to do next.

After graduation, I struggled to find my path. I spent days in bed, feeling aimless and confused. I know what it's like to feel uncertain without a clear vision for the future. This struggle led me to apply to any school that would accept me, eventually leading to partial online and on-campus studies.

I enrolled in a community college, still unsure of my career path, but I knew I wanted to continue my education. I took this time to challenge myself and attend school more frequently. I eventually learned how to become a transfer student. From there, I pursued a more specialized education in film.

Despite the challenges and uncertainty, I was able to carve out a vision for myself and make it a reality. I learned the importance of pursuing what truly mattered to me and not just following someone else's expectations. I realized that college was not the only path to success and that having a clear vision for one's future was essential.

Mistake to Avoid: A Life Without Vision

A person who lacks vision is like a wanderer, moving aimlessly without direction or purpose. Without a clear idea of where you're headed, every step feels uncertain, every choice riddled with doubt. Life becomes a series of reactions instead of intentional decisions, leading to confusion, frustration, and a sense of drifting without purpose.

When I lacked a vision for my future, especially regarding college, I found myself in this state. I didn't have a guiding principle to anchor me or a clear destination to work toward. Instead, I followed the flow of external expectations, applying to schools without understanding why or what I really wanted. This lack of clarity created feelings of hopelessness and frustration when things didn't go as planned. It wasn't until I started forming a vision of what I truly wanted—an education that aligned with my passions—that things began to shift.

Without a vision, you allow life to happen to you instead of actively shaping it. You end up living out someone else's plans or expectations, missing out on opportunities that align with your true desires and purpose. The danger of having no vision is that it leads to stagnation—you may be busy, but you're not moving forward toward something meaningful.

Having a clear vision is like possessing a compass. It doesn't just tell you what direction to go; it helps you make informed decisions along the way. It acts as a filter, allowing you to discern which paths are worth pursuing and which are distractions. It motivates you to get up each morning with a sense of purpose and determination, guiding your steps with intention.

When you avoid the mistake of living without vision, you empower yourself to lead a life of clarity and fulfillment. You no longer accept whatever comes your way; instead, you deliberately create the future you want. Vision is what turns dreams into actionable goals, and it's the driving force that allows you to overcome obstacles and setbacks with resilience.

Taking the First Step

Now is the time to envision boldly. Do not be afraid to dream big, even if your dream seems impossible right now. Remember, every great achievement began with a vision that seemed out of reach. The difference between those who achieve their dreams and those who don't is often as simple as taking that first step. And then the next. And the next. Your journey begins with a single, courageous moment of imagination—a moment where you allow yourself to see the life you truly want and commit to pursuing it with all your heart.

Take a deep breath, close your eyes, and ask yourself once more: What do you see for yourself? What does your best life look like? Begin to craft that vision today, knowing that it has the power to transform not just your own life but potentially the world around you.

Now, go deeper:

1. **Visualize in detail**: Begin by painting a vivid picture in your mind. Don't just stop at broad strokes—get specific. What does your day-to-day look like in this best version of your life? What are you doing when you wake up in the morning? Where are you? Who are you surrounded by? Let every detail become real in your imagination. The more you immerse yourself in these specifics, the more powerful your vision will become.

2. **Feel the emotions**: Vision alone is not enough. Connect emotionally with the life you see. Feel the excitement, the sense of fulfillment, the joy of achieving your goals. Let yourself experience these emotions fully as though this vision is your current reality. The more real it feels emotionally, the stronger the drive to turn that vision into reality.

3. **Write it down**: Take this vision out of your mind and put it into words. Writing solidifies thoughts and gives them structure. Write down not only what you see but also how it makes you feel. Revisit these words regularly. They'll serve as a compass to remind you of where you're headed when doubt creeps in or obstacles arise.

4. **Identify one action you can take today**: Dreams only become reality through action. Ask yourself, "What is one small step I can take today

toward this vision?" Don't focus on the whole journey, just the first step. Whether it's researching something new, reaching out to someone, or simply making a decision, that step forward sets your dream in motion.

5. **Commit to growth**: Understand that the vision you hold will evolve. As you grow, so will your dream. Stay open to the process, trusting that even when things don't seem to be going according to plan, they're still leading you toward the life you've envisioned.

2

Desire

To create the life of your dreams, it's important to first understand your deepest desires. When we break down the word "desire," it originates from the Latin word "desideri," which means to wish, long for, expect, or demand. The word "desider" is derived from the stars, and "sider" or "sidious" or "siderious" refers to heavenly bodies and star constellations.

What is it you long for? What are your expectations for your future? What do you aspire to be, do, or have?

Having delved into the etymology of the word "desire," we now possess a deeper understanding of what we truly long for. This heightened awareness guides our thoughts on the expectations we hold for the lives we are creating for ourselves.

The word "desire" is synonymous with "goal," which means 'purpose' or 'something one hopes or intends to accomplish' according to the Merriam-Webster dictionary.

One way to figure out your desires is to have a conversation with yourself. Look at what is possibly missing in your life, think about what you have wanted since you were young, and consider the people you admire and the things you aspire to. Put your ideas into action and consider what will bring you joy, help you grow, and build your character.

Here are some questions to consider:

- Will this bring me joy?
- Will this make me a better person?
- Will this help me grow?
- Can this make me money?
- Is this solving a problem for others?

If you see yourself getting excited or finding something missing, consider going for it.

Clarity! Be Clear about Your Desires

Once you have clarified your desires and answered the initial questions, take some time to write them down. Delve into detail, getting specific about what you want to have, do, or be. For the person you aspire to be, jot down possible characteristics, such as daily wardrobe, social circle, living arrangements, home, car, and relationship desires. If it's material possessions you yearn for, visualize and detail them. Consider how they will enhance your life and make you a better person and even how these things will help others around you. Think about the actions that will lead to your desires, considering the importance and worth of investing time and money into them. Keep the initial questions and statements in mind as you proceed.

Jot down your desires on sticky notes, small pieces of paper, or laminated index cards and place them in the places you frequent, whether at home, work, or your office. You can also save these notes on your phone to easily access them during your free time. Having these reminders in the places you frequent can remind yourself what you are working towards and what you hope to achieve. These reminders constantly reinforce your goals or desires, helping you stay focused and committed. By reading them frequently, you will continually be reminded of your mission for the day and the steps you need to take to move closer to your goal. This will provide the guidance and motivation to work towards your aspirations.

Notice how we use the word desire compared to "want." Desire signifies demand and expectation, while *want* is rooted in the concepts of deficiency, poverty, and deprivation, while "want" also encompasses the idea of 'desire' and 'wish.' It's important to recognize that "desire" does not carry the connotations of lacking or poverty but instead implies expectation. On the other hand, "want" includes the concept of 'desire' in its definition as something to be wished for.

When considering your desires, aim for something beyond yourself. Consider the long-term impact and the legacy you want to leave behind. By looking at the bigger picture, you can meet your needs and everything that matters to you. When you think about future generations and helping others, your all-encompassing desire will ensure that everything you need and value is cared for because you think beyond yourself.

The most significant step in achieving your desires is to believe they are attainable. Identify your desires and embrace them as part of your vision.

Research, Re-Search, RESEARCH!

Now, let's discuss researching your desire. Whether it's something you desire to be, have, or do, it's essential to learn some things about your desire. Understanding the background, origins, and purpose of your desire will give you a deeper connection and a better understanding of its significance. Consider taking personal photos or visiting the place you desire, if applicable. For example, if it's a car, go to a dealership and take it for a test drive. If it's a person or a profession you aspire to, engage in meaningful conversations with individuals already in that profession. Ask questions about what they enjoy about it and what led them to pursue it. The more you delve into your desires and understand them, the more they resonate with you. This deeper understanding will guide you in determining whether these desires truly align with your soul.

Have you ever struggled with staying committed to your goal?

My Story of How Desire with Clarity and Research Result Accomplishment

One key to staying committed is understanding exactly what your goal or desire entails. I faced a challenge with my own goal after college. I always thought I would move into my own home after graduating, but I didn't do enough research and I wasn't clear; therefore, my commitment wasn't strong enough. Due to me not preparing to move into my home after graduating from UCLA, my living situation at my mother's house became tense. I ended up moving in with my boyfriend and his relatives' home for four and a half years. My boyfriend and I had different desires concerning moving out of his relatives' home, which was one reason it took some years for us to get into our own place. Another reason was that we did not research the steps to get into our home.

This lack of clarity and research prevented us from finding common ground and moving out sooner. The turning point came when I was told I had to leave, which pushed me to take action. From sunrise to sunset, I spent 43 days in my car, getting clear on where I wanted to live and researched the location, apartment requirements, and job opportunities. The research allowed us to finally commit to the goal of living in our own home. On the forty-fourth day, we packed our van with all our belongings and moved to a new town.

Mistake to Avoid: Lack of Clarity and Research

Not having clarity nor researching will make your goal and vision tough to stay committed to. When you aren't clear about what you truly want or fail to research the necessary steps to achieve it, your desire becomes shaky, and your commitment falters. Without clarity, you can't visualize the end result, which makes it harder to stay motivated, especially when challenges arise.

I learned this the hard way after college. I had the desire to move into my own home, but my lack of preparation and clear vision prevented me from taking the necessary actions to make it happen. I hadn't done the research—where I wanted to live, what I needed to do to get there, or how much it would cost. I had an idea, but it wasn't specific enough. As a result, my commitment to the goal was weak, and when things got tough, I found myself living with my boyfriend and his relatives for years longer than I had planned.

Without clarity, it's easy to get lost in the process. The desire may be there, but the lack of direction causes delays, confusion, and frustration. You find yourself wandering aimlessly, wondering why things aren't falling into place. For me, the turning point came when I was pushed out of my comfort zone. Being told I had to leave my current living situation forced me to face the reality of my unclear goal. It wasn't until I spent time reflecting and researching that I gained the clarity I needed to move forward.

Research is equally important. It's what transforms a vague dream into a concrete, achievable plan. When my boyfriend and I finally started researching apartment options, job opportunities, and housing requirements, things began to shift. Research provided the roadmap we needed, and from that moment on, our commitment strengthened. We knew exactly what steps to take, and our desire became a well-defined goal.

The mistake of not having clarity or doing research is a common pitfall when pursuing a desire. It leaves you vulnerable to distractions, delays, and ultimately, disappointment. When you aren't clear, you'll find it harder to persevere because you can't see the finish line. When you don't research, you lack the practical knowledge to make informed decisions, leading to wasted time, energy, and resources.

Avoiding this mistake means taking the time to get clear on your desire. Ask yourself: What do I truly want? What does success look like for me? Once you have that clarity, dive into the research. Find out what steps are required, who can help you, and what potential obstacles might arise. The combination of clarity and research ensures that your desire is not just a fleeting wish but a well-thought-out plan that you can commit to wholeheartedly.

Your Next Step

The key to achieving your desire is having clarity and researching to know what you are embarking on. One common mistake people make is not fully understanding their desires. When it came to living independently, we had to figure out how to make it work, including financial planning and resources. Our research was not just about the location but also the process. It's about pulling resources together and utilizing them wisely. The crucial steps are getting clear on your desire and doing research ahead of time; otherwise, your circumstances will push you to make sure you figure out what you need to know about your desire.

Let's break this down:

1. **Clarify your desire**: Clarity is essential. You cannot move toward something you cannot clearly see. Ask yourself: What exactly do I care for having? Don't settle for vague or broad desires like "I want success" or "I want to be happy." Define what success or happiness looks like for you. Is it financial independence, a particular career, a specific lifestyle? What do you care for your life to look like in detail? Get crystal clear on this, because a hazy vision leads to hazy results.

2. **Identify the essential elements**: Once you've clarified your desire, break it down into components. What are the key elements you

need to know about? For example, if you're aiming to live independently, it's not just about finding a place to live. It's about understanding the costs, logistics, and responsibilities that come with that. What resources—financial, emotional, or educational—will you need to achieve this desire?

3. **Research wisely**: Information is power, but not just any information. Target your research toward the areas that directly influence your journey. If your goal involves finances, look into budgeting, credit, and investing. If it's about a career move, study your field, identify the required skills, and learn about potential obstacles. Your research becomes your roadmap, showing you where to start, what to avoid, and how to navigate challenges.

4. **Leverage available resources**: You don't have to figure everything out alone. Use the resources around you—people, books, tools, and mentors. Take advantage of the expertise others have gained, and don't hesitate to ask for help or guidance when you need it. The more prepared you are, the smoother the path will be.

5. **Prepare or be pushed**: If you don't take the time to prepare in advance, life will force you to. You might find yourself scrambling to learn things at the last minute, often in stressful or challenging situations. By doing the groundwork

ahead of time, you empower yourself to handle what comes with more ease and confidence. Preparation is a proactive investment in your future success, not just a box to check.

PART 2 - DO

Engage in the joy of using your imagination, applying principles, and deliberately harnessing your subconscious mind. Learn from others, think beyond yourself, harness the power of your thoughts and words, and know when to pivot. 'DO' means "to perform, execute, achieve, carry out, or bring to pass by the procedure of any kind."

3

Imagination

What is Imagination?

When we look at the definition of 'imagination,' it means "faculty of the mind that manipulates images," when we get down to the etymology of imagination, the stem 'imaginari' means to "form an image." Let's look at "image." In Latin, the image comes from "imaginem" meaning 'copy, imitation, likeness, statue, picture."

Now is the time to unleash your imagination.

This is your chance to imagine exactly what you want to be, do, and have in the objective world. Start by crafting a narrative. Develop the story of this person using the questions in the chapter where you identified your desires. Then, gather images from various sources like books, magazines, newspapers, and online articles to create a vision board for yourself. Make it large enough to see daily, whether on a cardboard box or your office or room wall. Utilize images of other people doing the things you aspire to do or of the things you wish to have. Arrange the images in a collage that you can also carry with you on your phone. Additionally, create a digital version of this collage for your laptop or desktop so that you can view it daily. Use the information from the articles to start your research. This involves going online, visiting the library, reading books, and learning about the person you want to become or the things you want to have.

For example, if you're interested in becoming a mechanical engineer, find out the necessary classes and equipment needed. If you want to travel to another country, learn everything you can about it. Same goes for a road trip – plan the route and connect with individuals who can provide valuable insight. If you have a specific car in mind, research its history and technical details. Finally, talk to people who may have connections to the person you admire or who have experience in the areas you're interested in pursuing. Seek their wisdom and advice to guide you on the right path.

The imagination is an incredible tool. It is one of our mental faculties and operates phenomenally. The brain knows no difference between what is real and what is imagined. For example, studies show that parts of the brain will light up in an imagined scenario as if the scenario were real.

Bird's Eye View vs First Person Perspective

When delving deep into your imagination, it's important to consider how you visualize yourself. Sometimes, we see ourselves from a bird's-eye view or in the third person. Seeing ourselves from the perspective of another individual. Instead of visualizing yourself from a third-person perspective, try visualizing yourself in the first-person. Imagine yourself being, doing, and having the things you desire. This helps to feed your subconscious mind with the reality you want to create. The subconscious mind, just like the brain, doesn't differentiate between what's real and what's not, so when you see yourself in first person, it's as if you're looking through your own eyes, as you do in the objective world. Visualize the world you want to see for yourself. Use your senses to make your imagination even more real (see, smell, taste, sound, and touch). This takes practice, but repetition makes it easier, like learning an instrument or riding a bike.

Your Brain on Imagination

Many people overlook the importance of understanding how their brains and minds function. It is often assumed that imagination is only for children, but in reality, there is a structure in our brain called the hippocampus. Your imagination functions from a part of your hemisphere of the brain called the hippocampus, which is located in the temporal lobe. Additionally, stress can significantly impact our brain structures, such as the hippocampus and amygdala, where your emotional responses function. This can lead to the atrophy of the imagination. It's important to be mindful of what we are exposed to, as our imagination plays a crucial role in how we perceive the world around us. The way to heal the brain or repair it is through music. Listening to or playing music lights up many brain parts, including the hippocampus and amygdala. Studies show that music can repair damaged tissues in the brain with its beats, rhythm, and tones, which activate the amygdala (where our emotional responses function) and the right hippocampus (where our spatial memory, visual, and imagination functions). Let's be more intentional about what we subject ourselves to and take the time to nurture our imagination.

My Imagination Story

While in my fourth month at film school, I made up my mind that after graduation, I would go back to community college and eventually transfer to UCLA. I was determined, even though it seemed like a distant goal at the time.

After finishing film school, I volunteered on a UCLA student film, working in the prop department. For three hours, I guarded the prop bin on UCLA's campus. As I stood there, I allowed my imagination to take over. I started telling myself stories: "UCLA was the only school I applied to, and I got in." I could see it so clearly in my mind. I didn't just think it—I believed it, felt it, lived it in my imagination.

With this vision in mind, I enrolled back into community college, repeating that same story to myself: "I'm going to UCLA. I belong there." I joined a student transfer program that gave me the opportunity to visit UCLA's campus on Saturdays once or twice a quarter for various events. Each time I set foot on campus, I would imagine myself as a student already there. I would walk through the different buildings, telling myself, "I'm going to class in this building, and next, I have a lecture in that one."

When I returned home, I continued my imaginative journey. I pictured myself walking across the campus with other students, feeling the sun on my face, the weight of my backpack on my shoulders. I immersed myself in these stories until they felt as real as the ground beneath my feet.

The following spring, just four days before my 24th birthday, my vision became reality—I was accepted to UCLA. But my imagination didn't stop there. I immediately began to visualize myself graduating, holding my degree, feeling the pride and joy of accomplishment. I saw myself walking across the stage, hearing the applause, and feeling that rush of fulfillment.

Through the power of imagination, I created a vision so strong it manifested itself into reality. My journey to UCLA wasn't just about applying to a school; it was about believing deeply in a story I told myself, again and again, until it became my truth.

After two straight years of college with no breaks (the only time I took a break was when the schools were closed for holidays), I put my body under serious stress to finish school. The following year, I found myself in emergency rooms six (6) times because I felt the stress pains throughout my entire body.

While living with my boyfriend and his relatives, I had challenges tapping into my imagination. In the last two years of living with them, I started back playing trombone (an instrument I picked up the last couple weeks of my junior year in high school) and singing. In my last year living with my boyfriend's relatives, I imagined him and myself in our own one-bedroom apartment.

During our last forty-three days of living with his relatives, from sunup to sundown (during the 2020 pandemic), I would stay in our car, creating our new home in a new town in my imagination. On the forty-fourth day, our van was fully packed with just about all our things, and we got on the road and headed to our new town and new home.

Mistake to Avoid: Neglecting the Power of Imagination

Not using one of your most powerful mental faculties, the imagination, could possibly rob you of great opportunities you could create for yourself. Imagination is a tool that allows you to mentally construct your future before it happens. It's the bridge between where you are and where you want to be. Without it, you're stuck in the limitations of your current reality, unable to see beyond the obstacles in front of you.

When you neglect your imagination, you limit your ability to dream, visualize, and bring forth new possibilities. Instead of thinking beyond your circumstances, you stay confined within them. You miss out on the chance to envision a better future, whether it's landing your dream job, finding the perfect place to live, or reaching a personal goal. Without the practice of using imagination, your mind is less open to new ideas and opportunities that could transform your life.

For me, using my imagination allowed me to create a vivid mental image of attending UCLA long before it became a reality. I could see it, feel it, and believe it so strongly that my actions aligned with that vision. If I hadn't tapped into my imagination, I might have settled for less, thinking it was too far out of reach or impossible. But because I envisioned myself there, my belief grew stronger, and I stayed committed to taking the necessary steps.

Imagination works hand-in-hand with desire and vision. It helps you clarify your goals and keeps you motivated when times are tough. Without it, you're left to rely solely on logic and what already exists in your current environment. This can lead to missed opportunities because you're only seeing life as it is, not as it could be.

By not engaging your imagination, you also limit your ability to solve problems creatively. When challenges arise, imagination allows you to think outside the box and come up with innovative solutions. Without it, you may get stuck in frustration, unable to find a way forward. Your dreams remain unfulfilled, not because they're impossible, but because you couldn't see yourself achieving them.

The beauty of imagination is that it gives you permission to explore limitless possibilities. It allows you to dream big, break free from the constraints of your current circumstances, and believe in outcomes that haven't yet materialized. Without it, you lose the opportunity to create the life you truly want. You end up accepting less than you deserve because you can't see beyond the immediate challenges.

Don't make the mistake of neglecting this powerful mental faculty. Imagination is where ideas are born, plans are created, and desires start to come alive. When you actively use it, you open the door to opportunities that otherwise might have gone unnoticed. Imagination not only helps you see what's possible but also gives you the confidence and motivation to pursue it with everything you have.

Next Step

Start by finding a quiet place for at least five minutes to take an inventory of your visualization or imagery abilities. Can you visualize yourself in the first person? Can you recreate images you have seen or read about? If you aren't able to tap into your imagination, take some time to listen or make music. Music may help jog old memories and even help you produce new ones (listen to some joyful and uplifting lyrics). Practice imagining daily, and soon, imagining yourself as desired will become second nature.

Let's explore this further:

1. **Begin with stillness**: Imagination flourishes in moments of calm. Find a space where you can sit quietly, away from distractions, for just a few minutes each day. In this quiet space, focus on becoming aware of your ability to visualize. Ask yourself: When I close my eyes, can I see a clear picture of something or someone? Can I place myself into a scenario, as if I'm living it right now? Don't judge yourself if this feels difficult at first. The act of noticing is the first step.

2. **Assess your imagery skills**: Visualization comes more naturally to some than others. You might find that you can imagine places, people, and experiences vividly, or you may realize that your mental images are fuzzy. Either way, start where you are. If you're struggling to create

images, use memory as a tool. Think of a place you've been or a moment that made you feel joyful. How clearly can you recreate that scene in your mind? The more you practice, the stronger your imagery skills will become.

3. **Use music as a bridge**: Imagination isn't limited to visual images; it's deeply connected to emotion. Music can evoke emotions and memories that help bring your imagination to life. When you listen to joyful or uplifting music, pay attention to the feelings and images that arise. Do certain songs transport you to specific memories or places? Use this emotional connection as fuel for your imagination. You can even visualize scenes that match the mood or lyrics of a song, allowing the music to guide your mind's eye.

4. **Practice daily**: Just like any skill, imagination grows stronger with practice. Set aside a few minutes each day to imagine. Start small—perhaps by visualizing yourself successfully completing a task or seeing yourself in a peaceful setting. As this becomes easier, challenge yourself to imagine bigger, more complex scenes: What does your ideal day look like? What version of yourself are you becoming? With time, this daily practice will feel more natural, and imagining the life you desire will flow effortlessly.

5. **Immerse yourself in your imagination**: Don't just visualize yourself as an outside observer. Engage all your senses and see the world from the first-person perspective. How do things smell, taste, and sound in your ideal scenario? What emotions come up? The deeper you immerse yourself in these visualizations, the more real they will feel, making it easier to move toward these visions in your everyday life.

4

Power of Thoughts and Words

Our Thoughts Live

Our thoughts play a crucial role in achieving our desires. Thoughts are vibrational energy. A Universal Law called the Law of Vibrations states that everything vibrates, nothing rests. Our thoughts are included. We've heard of 'thought waves.' A wave vibrates

Often, our actions and repeated thoughts are closely linked. As we continue to focus on certain thoughts, they gradually seep into our subconscious minds, as discussed in the previous chapter. The subconscious mind is expansive and absorbs everything, ultimately manifesting our repeated thoughts into reality. Therefore, it is essential to be mindful of our thoughts and their alignment with our desires. Our thoughts are like seeds, and our minds are tied to the soil, nurturing positive and productive thoughts. If our thoughts do not align with our goals, addressing and redirecting them is crucial. We must be intentional in our thoughts, as they have the power to shape our realities. Remember the importance of focusing on positive, constructive thoughts manifesting our desires into actions and reality. I'm here to help you shift your mindset and understand the importance of our thoughts in creating the life we truly desire.

My Thought Experience

In high school, I used to think I wasn't smart enough to attend any UCs (University of California schools - research institutions). This thought shaped my words and actions, ultimately leading to rejection. Have you ever experienced similar challenges where negative thoughts prevented you from achieving something? This was my experience. However, four years later, I changed my mindset. I went from believing I couldn't attend any UCs to believing I could get into UCLA. As a result, everything started falling into place. I had to shut out all opposing thoughts that weren't benefitting me from getting into UCLA. The most common mistake people make is not filtering the information they consume, which greatly influences our thoughts and ideas. Therefore, it's important to read books or listen to individuals who align with our desired goals, i.e., take on the mindset of those whose goals align with ours. By shaping our thoughts to match those of the people we admire, we can ultimately shape our subconscious minds, words, and actions accordingly.

Our Words Are Mightier Than a Sword

In earlier chapters, we discussed the etymology of WORDS and their origins to understand how to use them appropriately when expressing ourselves. Words carry great power; if we are not mindful of our language, we may unintentionally attract or manifest things we do not desire. When you clearly define what the meaning of a word is, you begin to use it in its proper form. People may be more willing to use words in their proper and literary context when they know the word's origin.

Words are deeply linked to our thoughts. As you continue reading, you will realize how carefully chosen words can help manifest your desires or unintentionally bring about what you do not want. Focusing on what you desire and care to do, be, and have is crucial. When we dwell on what we do not want, those thoughts and words have a way of coming back to us.

Understanding the origin of words, many of which stem from Latin, can help us use them more effectively in creating our desired reality. By learning the true meanings and origins of our words, we can come one step closer to manifesting what we truly desire.

Life and Death Spoken

The Bible provides a profound example of the impact of words in Proverbs 18:21, "life and death are in the power of the tongue." What we speak can shape our reality. When we talk about others, we may inadvertently speak about ourselves. It's a reminder that our words can have a lasting impact, for better or worse. Other sayings echo this sentiment, such as "The pen is mightier than the sword." The words we write and speak have the potential to cut deeper than any weapon. It's important to remember that our words have the power to build up or tear down. Words have the ability to shape ideas and create entire worlds. Consider a movie script - it starts with words on a page but then is brought to life by a collaborative group of individuals. Similarly, a play is born from a playwright's words and acted out by a group of people. Even the words you are reading now in this book have been carefully crafted to influence and empower you. The power of our words cannot be understated, as they can be wielded for both creation and destruction.

My Words Experience

While attending film school in Los Angeles, I decided to apply only to UCLA. I chose UCLA because I thought I wasn't smart enough in high school to attend, and I believed my SAT scores and GPA were not up to par. As a result, I did not get accepted to any colleges. I realized that the words I used to express my doubts about my intelligence significantly impacted the outcome.

It took me two years after starting film school to change my mindset and decide that I could attend a UC. That shift in perspective led me to be intentional with my words, speaking only of my desire to attend UCLA. This deliberate focus on what I genuinely cared for led to my acceptance despite the doubts expressed by others.

I learned that our words have the power to shape our reality, for better or for worse. It's important to be mindful of the words we use and to be intentional in expressing our desires. We should avoid speaking about what we don't want or desire without countering it with what we truly care for. By intentionally aligning our words with our desires, we can powerfully manifest our goals.

Mistake to Avoid: Misusing Your Thoughts and Words

When we are not intentional with our thoughts and words, we might create worlds for ourselves that we really don't want to live in. Both thoughts and words are incredibly powerful—they act as the architects of our reality. If we misuse them, consciously or unconsciously, we may find ourselves trapped in situations that don't align with our true desires.

Thoughts, the seeds of our internal world, shape the beliefs we hold about ourselves and the world around us. They guide our perceptions, influence our actions, and set the course for what we believe is possible. If our thoughts are filled with doubt, fear, or negativity, those same patterns will reflect in our external experiences. The problem arises when we don't recognize the role our thoughts play in creating our circumstances. Instead of seeing them as the root cause of our struggles, we often place the blame on external situations.

In my own experience, my negative thoughts about not being smart enough to attend any UC schools blocked me from even trying. My thoughts shaped my actions, or rather, my inactions. I didn't apply to the right schools or put in the effort because, deep down, I didn't believe it was possible for me. That lack of belief manifested into reality. For years, I lived in a world where rejection and disappointment were the norms—not because I wasn't capable, but because my thoughts and beliefs didn't allow me to see another outcome.

Similarly, our words are the tools we use to bring those internal thoughts into the external world. Words have creative power—they can either reinforce our desires or perpetuate our doubts. When we speak, we declare our beliefs and intentions to the universe, setting things in motion. If our words reflect self-doubt or negativity, we give life to those beliefs. We affirm our fears and make them more concrete. Over time, this can shape a reality we don't actually want to live in, yet it becomes difficult to escape because we've verbally reinforced it.

For example, I spoke about my doubts regarding attending UCLA for years. I would say things like, "I'm not smart enough to go there," or "I won't get accepted with my grades." These words cemented my feelings of inadequacy and ultimately prevented me from applying to other schools with confidence. It was only after I consciously chose to change my language and start speaking words of possibility—saying, "I'm going to UCLA"—that the doors began to open.

When we aren't deliberate about the words we use, we unintentionally align ourselves with the things we fear rather than the things we desire. Words like "I can't," "I'm not good enough," or "That's not for me" build walls that limit us from seeing or seizing new opportunities. Our words become self-fulfilling prophecies, shaping a world of limitations instead of one filled with potential.

The real danger lies in not being aware of this power. When we are careless with our thoughts and words, we unintentionally create a reality that doesn't reflect what we truly want. We end up feeling stuck, frustrated, or defeated, all the while not realizing that we've had the power to change it all along. The more we repeat these negative thoughts and words, the deeper we become entrenched in a reality that feels out of alignment with our true desires.

To avoid this, we must become intentional. We need to train our minds to think thoughts that align with what we truly want, and we need to speak words that affirm those desires. Just as negative thoughts and words create barriers, positive ones can create breakthroughs. By intentionally focusing on thoughts of success, joy, and possibility—and speaking them into existence—we can shape a world that mirrors our highest aspirations.

Next Step

This step is to be clear about what you genuinely desire and then use your thoughts and words to affirm and manifest those desires. Take the time to understand the origins of your words, as this can help you better align them with your intentions. Be intentional with your thoughts. Your words and your thoughts have the power to evoke your desires and shape your reality, so be mindful in using them.

Let's break this down further:

1. **Clarity is essential**: Before anything else, get crystal clear on what you desire. Vague desires lead to vague outcomes. Whether it's something material, emotional, or spiritual, take the time to explore your true desires. Ask yourself: What is it that I really want? Why do I want it? The clearer you are about your goals, the more focused your thoughts and words will become in helping you reach them.

2. **Thoughts are the foundation**: Your thoughts create the mental environment in which your desires can grow. Pay attention to the thoughts you allow to occupy your mind. Are they supportive of your goals, or are they full of doubt, fear, and negativity? If negative thoughts arise, recognize them without judgment, and

replace them with positive, affirming thoughts. Train your mind to focus on possibilities and solutions rather than problems and limitations.

3. **Intentional language**: Words hold energy and power. Every word you speak either moves you closer to or further away from what you want. Be conscious of the language you use, both when speaking to others and in your self-talk. For example, instead of saying, "I can't," say, "I'm working on it." Instead of, "This is impossible," say, "I'm finding a way." Choose words that affirm your belief in your ability to achieve your desires.

4. **Words as affirmations**: Use your words to affirm what you want. Whether through daily affirmations or simply speaking positively about your goals, your words can reinforce your intentions. For example, if your desire is to find more peace in your life, you might affirm, "I am surrounded by peace and calm in every area of my life." Speak as though your desires are already unfolding. Your words create a frequency that aligns with what you seek.

5. **Understand the origins of your language**: Consider where your words and thought patterns come from. Often, we unknowingly carry limiting beliefs and negative language from past experiences, environments, or other people's opinions. Reflect on the roots of your

thoughts and words. If they're not aligned with your highest desires, make a conscious decision to shift them. Understanding this will allow you to reclaim the power of your words and align them with your goals.

6. **Daily practice**: The power of thoughts and words lies in consistency. Make it a daily habit to be intentional with both. Start each morning by setting positive intentions, choosing affirming thoughts, and speaking encouraging words. With practice, you will find that your mindset naturally shifts, and your reality begins to reflect the power of your thoughts and words.

5

Subconscious Mind and the "How"

In previous chapters I briefly discuss the subconscious mind. Let's go deeper in this one. In this chapter I explain the importance of the subconscious mind in attracting our true desires. Our minds are like soil, and our thoughts are like seeds. This means that whatever thoughts we plant in our minds, whether good or bad, will ultimately determine what we harvest. Like watering seeds, our continuous thoughts nurture and grow them into roots, eventually into actions. Our conscious and subconscious minds act as the soil, and the consistency of our thoughts becomes the water that keeps the seeds growing. It's crucial to be mindful of our thoughts, as they can manifest into actions and, eventually, habits. By focusing on positive thoughts, we attract the things we desire, but when we dwell on negativity, we unintentionally attract and act upon what we don't want. Therefore, it's important to be mindful of our thoughts and tend to the seeds we plant in our minds.

The foundation of manifestation lies in our subconscious mind, one of several minds that function differently within us. As we go about our daily lives, our conscious mind forms our thoughts, while our subconscious mind, present from birth, operates continuously. Our subconscious mind takes shape between the ages of zero to five or six, shaping our thoughts, intellect, reasoning, and willpower based on the influences of our environment, guardians, relatives, and experiences. The subconscious mind has the ability to remember everything and shape your reality.

Subconscious Mind is the HOW

Our subconscious mind internalizes every detail, regardless of whether it is positive or negative. Our spoken and unspoken thoughts eventually become the essence of our subconscious mind, attracting vibrations that align with our internalized beliefs. The body reflects these vibrations, attracting experiences and occurrences that resonate with our subconscious programming. Thus, our forgotten or even fleeting thoughts and words become embedded within our subconscious, shaping our life experiences. All that the subconscious mind takes in and is impressed upon is the HOW that makes everything for your desire to come to reality.

One challenge we face is the conflicting messages we allow ourselves to absorb. Have you ever wondered why something you long for seems out of reach? I have experienced this myself. Upon discovering the power of the subconscious mind and its ability to absorb and process our thoughts and experiences, I realized that I was attracting things that resonated with past negative experiences and repetitive thoughts, such as attending a four-year university. Through affirmations and visualizations, I started manifesting my true desires, such as attending UCLA, the only university I applied to as a transfer student. This shift in mindset, even before understanding the subconscious mind, allowed me to take action and see tangible results.

Be Surprise About HOW Things Come Together For You

Another major challenge people have is worrying about "HOW" things are going to come together for their desire. Have you had this challenge?

Many people are too afraid to pursue their desires because they are stuck in this exact cycle. They worry endlessly about "how" things will unfold. They want guarantees, a clear path, and a step-by-step plan before they even begin to move toward their dreams. But here's the secret: if we let go of our obsession with the "how" and take action anyway, we often find that things unfold in ways we couldn't have predicted.

Instead of being trapped by the need to control every detail, we must trust our subconscious mind to guide us. The subconscious mind is an incredibly powerful force. It can process information beyond our conscious understanding and align us with the right people, opportunities, and circumstances to help us achieve our goals. It works quietly in the background, organizing events and situations in ways we might not even notice.

Think of your subconscious mind like a gardener. When you plant a seed, you don't worry about how every single element in the soil will interact to make the seed grow. You simply plant it, water it, and trust that nature will take care of the rest. The same applies to your desires. Plant the seed of intention in your subconscious mind and let it handle the "how."

It's crucial to leave the "how" as an open question and allow things to unfold naturally, taking action only when it feels right.

Powerful lesson: the "how" is not always our concern. When we release our need for control and trust in our subconscious mind, we open ourselves to limitless possibilities. We begin to see opportunities where we once saw obstacles, and we find paths where we once saw dead ends. Remember, the subconscious mind is like a creative partner in your journey, constantly working behind the scenes to align everything in your favor.

My Subconscious Mind and the "HOW" Experience

One of the most significant challenges I faced when pursuing my desires was worrying about "how" things will come together. I used to be so focused on the "how" that it often paralyzed me from taking any meaningful action. I felt like I needed to know every step in the journey before even beginning. I became so obsessed with figuring out every detail that I didn't allow myself to dream freely or move toward my goals.

However, as I look back on certain moments in my life, I realize that the "how" was often taken care of by my subconscious mind. When I decided to transfer to UCLA, I unknowingly left the "how" to my subconscious. I had no idea how I would get in, how I would manage the application process, or even how I would afford it. Yet, I chose to believe in my desire and let go of the need to control every step.

Whenever I focused on my desires without obsessing over the "how," they often came to fruition in unexpected and remarkable ways. I found that trying to figure out the "how" is often the hardest part, and I have learned to do my best not to get caught up in it.

When I was younger, I would have spent countless hours worrying about "how" to get into UCLA, the only school I applied to, or "how" I would find the money to pay for it. But this time, I chose differently. I didn't worry.

I focused on my vision, trusted my subconscious mind, and took steps as they felt necessary. And in the end, things happened in ways I could never have imagined— better than I could have planned.

After all the imagining, aligning my thoughts and speaking my desire into my reality, I was accepted into UCLA (the only school I applied to) and only took out a small loan. The rest of my tuition, room and board were taken care of. Also, the small loan I took out was "paid back" (someHOW).

Mistake to Avoid: Not Filtering Input

The subconscious mind is constantly absorbing information, processing thoughts, emotions, and external stimuli, whether we are aware of it or not. It acts as the engine behind the scenes, working tirelessly to manifest the reality we live in based on the information we allow into it. If we are not careful about what we feed our subconscious—whether through thoughts, words, what we watch, or the people we surround ourselves with—it will manifest outcomes based on this unfiltered input. The "how" of our lives, the way circumstances unfold, is directly influenced by the contents of our subconscious mind.

When we neglect to intentionally direct our subconscious, it starts to work with whatever input it receives. It doesn't filter out negative thoughts or unwanted suggestions on its own—it simply takes in everything and shapes our reality accordingly. If we allow doubts, fears, limiting beliefs, or the negativity of others to fill our minds, we give those things the power to control the "how" of our lives. This often leads to undesired outcomes, situations that feel out of our control, and circumstances that leave us feeling trapped or stuck.

For example, if we constantly think, "I don't know how I'll ever afford this" or "I'm not smart enough," the subconscious mind accepts these thoughts as truths. It then begins to create experiences that align with these beliefs. Instead of opening doors or finding unexpected opportunities, it closes them, reinforcing the negative perceptions we've allowed in. You may find yourself missing out on chances simply because your subconscious was programmed to believe they weren't possible.

When you shift your focus to your desires and trust your subconscious mind, it starts to work on the 'how' for you. Just like when I imagined myself at UCLA, without obsessing over the details, my subconscious began aligning everything in my favor. Instead of worrying about how I would get accepted or how I would afford it, I focused on my vision. As a result, the pieces started falling into place—my acceptance to UCLA, the unexpected financial support, and even the repayment of my loan. This is the power of your subconscious mind when it's intentionally aligned with your desires. By letting go of the need to control every step, you open yourself up to unexpected and remarkable results.

The key takeaway is this: *if we don't purposefully direct our subconscious mind, we risk letting the "how" of life take shape based on random, unfiltered input.* This often results in unwanted circumstances that seem beyond our control. The subconscious mind is neutral; it simply brings into reality whatever it is fed. That's why it's essential to be mindful of the thoughts, ideas, and beliefs we consistently entertain, as they influence the "how" in ways we may not realize.

By filling your subconscious with empowering, positive thoughts and focusing on your desired outcomes, you train it to find solutions, open doors, and align circumstances in your favor. But if you leave it to chance, feeding it a mix of uncertainty, fear, and doubt, the "how" will reflect those things, often leading to results that do not serve you.

In short, be intentional with what you allow your subconscious mind to absorb. Your thoughts, words, and beliefs are the seeds, and the subconscious is the soil. Whether those seeds grow into the life you desire or into a garden full of weeds depends entirely on the quality of what you plant.

Your Next Step

The subconscious mind is often overlooked but holds the key to unlocking our true desires. In this age of information, we have the opportunity to explore and understand the power of the subconscious mind. It is crucial to take the time to reflect on the repetitive thoughts that have not benefited us and address the root causes of our challenges. We can align our thoughts and actions with what we genuinely desire by rewriting our negative experiences and consistently focusing on our true desires through affirmations and visualization. This deliberate practice will allow our bodies to resonate at the frequency of our true desires.

Don't get caught up in the "how." Just set your intention, plant your seed, and let the power of your subconscious mind work its magic. Believe that you are guided, trust in the process, and know that the universe is aligning things in ways you can't yet see. Your job is to keep moving forward, taking inspired action, and staying open to whatever comes next.

Here's the step you can take to activate the power of your subconscious mind:

1. **Identify and release limiting thoughts**: Begin by taking an honest inventory of the repetitive, negative thoughts that have been holding you back. These are the subconscious patterns that may be blocking your path to what you truly desire. Write them down, reflect on where they might be coming from, and acknowledge their presence. Once identified, consciously decide to let them go, knowing that they no longer serve you.

2. **Reprogram your mind through affirmations**: Now, replace those limiting beliefs with

empowering affirmations that align with your desires. For example, if you've been telling yourself, "I'm not capable," shift that to, "I am more than capable of achieving my desires." Say these affirmations aloud daily or write them out as often as you can. The more you repeat them, the more your subconscious mind will begin to accept them as truth.

3. **Practice visualization consistently**: Visualization is a powerful way to communicate with your subconscious mind. Spend a few minutes every day imagining yourself already living the life you desire. Engage all your senses—what does it look like, feel like, sound like, even smell like? The more real and vivid your visualizations are, the more your subconscious mind will begin to align your thoughts, actions, and opportunities to match that vision.

4. **Trust the process and stay open**: It's easy to get caught up in wanting to control every step of how your desires will manifest, but this can create resistance. Instead, focus on your intentions, take inspired actions when they present themselves, and trust that the universe and your subconscious mind are working together behind the scenes to bring your desires into reality. Let go of the "how," and stay open to unexpected ways your desires may unfold.

5. **Repeat daily**: The key to reprogramming your subconscious is consistency. The more regularly you affirm your desires, visualize them as your reality, and act in alignment with them, the more your subconscious will work to bring those desires to fruition. Over time, this practice will help you shift from old, limiting patterns to new, empowering ones that support the life you truly want.

6

Think Bigger Than You

Make An Impact

When thinking about your desires, whether it's something you want to accomplish, become, or own, make sure it goes beyond just benefiting yourself. What do you want to achieve or possess that can assist others? Think about what problems you can solve or what needs you can fulfill. Perhaps there's an issue you've personally experienced but haven't found a solution for - use this as an opportunity to create a solution that can help others facing the same challenge. If you're unsure about what issues exist or what problems need solving, take a deeper look at your own experiences and surroundings. Pay attention to conversations and interactions - is there something that others struggle with that you can offer a solution for? Many inventions and innovations have been born out of recognizing a need or a problem and creating a solution for it.

Consider what is lacking or needed in your community or society and think about how you can contribute to fulfilling those needs. Whether it's providing educational resources, creating new products, or offering solutions to existing problems, look for opportunities to make a positive impact and help others. By identifying and addressing the needs of others, you can not only achieve your own desires but also make a meaningful difference in the lives of those around you.

When you think beyond yourself, you have the potential to achieve more than if you had only considered your own desires. It's important that your desires can ultimately benefit others. Have you ever struggled with considering your goals' impact on others or thought about how you could use your achievements to assist people? When you think about your desires, it's important to take into account the effect they may have on others. Your vision should encompass the well-being of those around you and beyond. Remember that it can also positively impact others when you consider what you want to achieve, become, or have.

My Becoming a Godmother Experience

For example, four months into the film program, my good friend called to tell me that she was pregnant and that I was the Godmother. Immediately after getting off the phone with my good friend, I told myself, "I am attending UCLA." Two things happened to me at that moment. One, UCLA would be the only school I applied to, and two, I was going to school for my godchild. Making this about someone else propelled me to follow through with film school, going back and completing another year of community college, and applying and transferring to UCLA. Years later, I was able to help others in their college journeys by sharing my experiences.

In defining my desires, I asked myself how they could benefit others. Making this a part of my vision allowed me to expand my goals beyond personal fulfillment. I learned that by including others in my vision, I could also fulfill my own needs and gain a deeper understanding of what I may be lacking. It's important to think beyond simply working to pay our bills and consider how our choices can positively impact others in various ways.

Mistake to Avoid: Thinking Small

When you focus only on what *you* need or want, you might find that what you get in return often falls short. It's easy to make the mistake of centering your vision only around your personal desires. But when you don't consider how your actions and goals can impact others, you cut yourself off from a deeper sense of fulfillment and the opportunity to achieve even more than you initially thought possible. The truth is, when you create a vision that includes others, you tap into something bigger than yourself, which can lead to both your needs being met and helping those around you in a meaningful way.

Take my story, for example: When I found out that I was going to be a godmother, my entire outlook shifted.

It wasn't just about *me* anymore. In that moment, I made the decision that I was going to apply to UCLA. Not just for myself, but because I now had a responsibility to someone else—to my godchild. From that day forward, UCLA became the only school I applied to, and everything I did from then on wasn't just for my own benefit, but for theirs as well.

When I started thinking beyond my own needs, it gave me a stronger sense of purpose. It pushed me through film school, got me back into community college, and eventually led me to apply to UCLA and get accepted. This wasn't just about my dream anymore—it was about showing my godchild what was possible, setting an example, and being a source of inspiration and guidance in their life. By making it about someone else, I stayed focused, persistent, and determined, even when things got tough. And in the end, I achieved my goal.

So, ask yourself: *How can my vision impact others?* When you think bigger than yourself and include others in your goals, you'll find new levels of motivation. This not only helps you, but it also allows you to contribute positively to the lives of those around you. When your vision includes others, you gain a stronger sense of purpose and often find your own desires are fulfilled in the process.

If I had only focused on myself and what *I* wanted, I might not have pushed through. I might have given up when things got challenging. But thinking about how my success could benefit my godchild gave me the extra push

I needed. And the amazing thing? Years later, I was able to help others by sharing my experiences, guiding them on their own journeys to college. This ripple effect— helping others achieve their goals because I achieved mine—came about because my vision wasn't just about me.

When you limit your vision to only your personal desires, you can block opportunities that might otherwise come to you. Focusing only on yourself can leave you feeling like something is missing or like you're not getting what you truly want. But when you think bigger and consider how your goals can positively impact others, you open the door to receiving more than you ever imagined.

Ultimately, when you think beyond yourself, you not only meet your own needs, but you also create the opportunity to help others meet theirs. Your actions and success can inspire and uplift those around you, creating a cycle of positive impact that benefits everyone. So, don't make the mistake of thinking too small or too selfishly—expand your vision to include others, and watch how your goals unfold in ways that exceed your expectations.

Next Step

We often focus solely on personal gain, but I believe it's essential to consider how we can support others in their careers or help them solve problems. By being intentional about our desires, we can positively impact more people and break the cycle of routine thinking. It is crucial to ask ourselves, how can I benefit others? We aspire to be a source of support, provide guidance in life, and ultimately pay it forward.

The key is to see the bigger picture and consider how our achievements can benefit others. It's easy to overlook this, but once we realize that many people face similar challenges, we understand the importance of considering others. Doing so can create a cycle of support and enable others to help those around them. So, let us identify our desires and consider how we can support others on a larger scale. How can our achievements benefit others and empower them to do the same?

Here's the next step you can take to think beyond yourself and positively impact others:

1. **Reflect on your impact**: Take a moment to think about the ways your goals and actions can extend beyond your personal desires. Ask yourself: *How can my work, ideas, or achievements help others?* Identify one or two specific ways your personal success could support others in overcoming challenges, finding inspiration, or growing in their own journey. This could be through mentorship, sharing knowledge, or creating solutions that benefit others.

2. **Incorporate service into your goals**: As you set goals for yourself, add an element of service or contribution to your plans. For example, if

you're pursuing a career or project, ask: *How can this make life better for others?* Think about how you can use your unique skills or knowledge to create opportunities for others or provide support where it's needed.

3. **Start small, think big**: You don't have to make grand gestures right away. Start with small, intentional acts that positively impact those around you. Whether it's offering advice to a friend, supporting a colleague, or volunteering time for a cause, small actions add up. As you make these contributions, you'll develop a mindset that naturally seeks to think beyond your own needs and toward a larger purpose.

4. **Create a ripple effect**: Consider the long-term impact of your achievements. When you help someone, that person may go on to help others, creating a chain reaction of positive influence. Keep this in mind as you pursue your desires, knowing that every success you experience has the potential to lift others up. The more you focus on how your success benefits others, the more opportunities you will create for collective growth.

5. **Commit to ongoing reflection**: Regularly check in with yourself to ensure that you're continuing to think bigger than yourself. Ask: *How can I make a greater impact?* Look for ways to expand your influence, and challenge yourself to

think beyond immediate rewards. Over time, this approach will become a natural part of your mindset, leading to greater fulfillment in both your personal and communal achievements.

7

Principles from the Bible

In previous chapters I shared some of my experiences using Principles from the Bible. During my college journey, I didn't have anyone to show me the ropes of navigating college life. I went through much trial and error between 18 and 25 years old, attending 5 colleges and graduating from 2. Have you ever been challenged navigating through something you had no one to turn to for guidance? These three Bible verses helped me exponentially during my last 2 years of college. Use these principles for any journey you may embark upon.

Three Bible Scriptures

The Bible offers universal principles that can be applied by people of the Christian faith and beyond. James 2:17 teaches us that faith without works is dead. In other words, simply believing in something is not enough if it is not backed up by effort. When we have faith in a goal or desire but do not work towards it, our faith becomes meaningless. Habakkuk 2:2 encourages us to write down our visions and make them plain. Doing so reminds us of our aspirations and allows others to support us in achieving them. Ask, and it shall be given to you; seek, and you shall find it; knock, and the door will be open to you, as Luke 11:9 suggests, is an important part of receiving the answers we seek. Universal in nature, these verses guide us to combine faith with action, clarify our visions, seek the answers, and knock to get a door open, which are the efforts to be mindful. These principles apply to anyone who believes these principles work for them.

James 2:17

Let's take a closer look at each of these verses. James 2:17, "Faith without deeds is dead." Before we go any further, the etymology of "Faith" comes from the Latin word 'fides' which means "to trust, confidence, reliance, belief, credence," and later Latin "persuade." This verse is preached often and sometimes as a stand-alone verse. I've heard this verse so often coming up that I used it to help me achieve my goals. I interpret James 2:17 as faith, which is about believing in the possibility of something even if it hasn't been witnessed. When you have faith in something that has not yet materialized, you must bring it to fruition through action. You are actively learning and shaping the unseen into reality by taking steps, no matter how small.

Habakkuk 2:2

Passage of Habakkuk 2:2, "And the Lord answered me and said, Write the vision, and make it plain on tablets, that he may run that readeth it." This Scripture tells us we articulate our vision clearly when we write it down. By putting your thoughts on paper, you document and solidify your vision. Writing it down helps you remember and makes it accessible and easily comprehended. Write down your goal or desire in your own handwriting. Studies show that people remember the goals better when handwritten on paper than typed on a device. So when you think of your vision, write it down, and then see it, you essentially record it three times. This repetition is crucial because it moves the vision from your conscious mind to your subconscious mind, allowing it to manifest.

Luke 11:9

Luke 11:9, "And I say unto you, Ask and it shall be given you; seek, and ye shall find; knock, and it shall be opened unto you." This Scripture gives a three-in-one principle to utilize. The idea that if you ask, you shall receive is something we experience often. We follow the principle of asking and receiving when we seek an answer to our questions, whether a yes, no, maybe, or an explanation. Ms. Lauryn Hill beautifully expressed this in her song, "Forgive Them Father," on her *Miseducation of Lauryn Hill*. In her verse, she says, "If you're looking for the answer, then you gotta ask the question." Asking a question is like embarking on a quest, and the quest leads us to the answer we are searching for. So, when you pose questions about your desires, you will ultimately find the answers you seek. Asking the question is the first step in seeking something; when you receive the answer, you truly find it. Knock, and the door shall be open unto you is an act that will test your patience and perseverance. Every door you knock on may not open; however, a door will open for you. That is the door for you. Seek, and ye shall find, is another principle that also deals with perseverance. If you are looking for something, you will, sooner or later, find what you are looking for. Stay intentional about what you are searching for.

My Bible Principles Experience

The principles found in the Bible provide excellent guidance for achieving many goals. The principles mentioned in this chapter have helped me achieve my desires for school and personal growth when I lacked guidance. They helped me see what was possible and provided the necessary alignment to make decisions and pursue my desires. As I navigated through school, the guidance I received from counselors was sometimes insufficient. Not expressing my goals or vision also contributed to my lack of direction. Here are my personal experiences with each of these principles.

During my college journey, "Faith without deeds is dead" helped me understand the importance of having confidence in myself and taking action. I persistently took action, especially when I reminded myself of my desires and the principles that guided me during my schooling.

I wrote down my vision of attending UCLA and the year I would transfer there on a sticky note and put it on my closet door in my bedroom. I looked at that sticky note nearly every day, and I would tell myself, "I am attending UCLA" for two years.

While in summer school at UCLA, I heard about the main famous performance theater on campus. I went to the theater to see the inside of this beautiful theater; all the doors were locked. I walked through the hallway to the back of the theater building and found the atrium that led downstairs. I opened the door and "knocked on the door" of one of the offices. A woman opened it and asked me, "How may I help you?" I told her I wanted to see inside this beautiful performance theater I had heard about. She told me it was locked for the summer, but the House staff was hiring ushers for work-study, and if I was interested, I could apply on the spot. I applied and was hired a month later. This was my first paying job as an adult. I had one of my graduation ceremonies at my job and stayed as an employee after graduating. I was promoted to Assistant House Manager, House Manager at the smaller theaters on campus, and even took a photography position.

After seeing photos of my former high school classmates in other countries, I questioned, "When I travel out of the country, where will I go?" Years later, my teacher's assistant asked me, "Are you going to study abroad?" I truly forgot that I had asked myself about traveling. I responded, "No, because I don't want to stay another year or any longer in school to do it." My teacher's assistant did not take my "No" as my final answer. He then proceeded to tell me about the study abroad program he did. The following summer, I studied abroad in Paris, France. Ultimately, all that I sought after I found, or it eventually found me.

Mistake to Avoid: Not Utilizing the Guidance of Ancient Texts and Proverbs

As you navigate your personal and professional journey, it's easy to overlook the wisdom available to you through religious texts or ancient and modern proverbs. However, when we fail to use these powerful teachings, we miss out on invaluable guidance that can help us achieve our goals. It's not enough to simply know what these texts say—we must put them into action if we want to experience true growth and success.

For example, during my college journey, I relied heavily on the principle, "faith without deeds is dead." This wasn't just a comforting thought; it was a reminder that I needed to act with confidence and intention to manifest my desire to attend UCLA. I didn't just hope for things to work out. I wrote down my vision on a sticky note, placed it where I would see it every day, and took continuous action to align myself with that vision.

This wasn't unique to me—anyone can benefit from applying similar principles. Whether it's a proverb from your own faith, a motivational quote, or an ancient teaching, these sources of wisdom guide us in practical ways. They help us not only to envision what we want but to actively take steps toward making those visions a reality.

By making use of this wisdom, I was able to achieve something that once felt impossible: getting accepted to UCLA and finding opportunities to support myself through work-study. I knocked on doors, both literally and figuratively, and those doors opened because I had faith, but I also followed it with action.

Now, consider if I hadn't applied that principle to my life. If I had only thought about what I wanted but hadn't put in the work, I might have missed the opportunity to apply to UCLA or to secure my first paying job there. Without putting the guidance of "faith without deeds is dead" into practice, I may have never reached the goals I had set for myself.

This isn't just about Bible principles. Whatever your background or belief system, there are teachings that can guide you if you let them. Proverbs, sayings, or spiritual truths are there for us to use in our current situations, not just to be read or memorized. If we ignore their practical applications, we miss out on the chance to align ourselves with the deeper wisdom that could lead us toward success and fulfillment.

When we don't incorporate these teachings into our everyday decisions, we risk wandering through life without clear direction. By not tapping into this ancient wisdom, we may overlook the exact guidance we need to achieve our goals or to avoid common mistakes. It's like having a map in front of us but refusing to follow it—we may get lost, delayed, or never reach our destination.

So, whether you draw wisdom from the Bible, the Quran, Buddhist teachings, or modern motivational thought, the key is to use it. These texts aren't just historical or religious artifacts—they are tools for us to apply to our lives today. By using them to shape your thoughts, guide your decisions, and inspire your actions, you can access a path of growth and purpose that leads to the fulfillment of your desires.

Remember, it's not enough to know the wisdom—we must live it. When you put these principles into action, as I did in my own journey, you'll find that doors open, opportunities arise, and the things you seek often come to you in ways that are far beyond what you could have planned.

Next Step

I encourage others to use these principles and take action, as they can help guide and empower you to pursue your desires. Using these principles is not just about reading them but actively applying them and taking the necessary steps to reach your goals. By utilizing these principles, you will find they work and can lead you to results. I recommend using the principles outlined in this chapter as a catalyst to guide you in your next steps. When you do so, you will see its impact on your performance.

Here's the step to help you apply these principles in your journey, whether from the Bible or other ancient texts:

1. **Select a guiding text that resonates with you**: Whether from the Bible or other ancient wisdom texts, find a passage or principle that speaks to your current life situation. You don't need to belong to a specific religion to benefit from these teachings; many sacred writings from various traditions offer timeless wisdom that can be applied universally. Look for a text that provides clarity, guidance, or inspiration for where you are in your journey.

2. **Reflect on the meaning of the text**: Once you've chosen a passage, spend some time reflecting on its meaning. How does it apply to your desires and your next steps? Whether it's a Bible verse like James 2:17 that speaks to the importance of action, or a proverb from another tradition, take time to meditate on how this wisdom can guide your actions and help you move forward with purpose.

3. **Write your vision and pair it with your chosen principle**: Just as Habakkuk 2:2 encourages us to "write the vision," take time to

write down your goals or dreams. Then, pair your vision with the principle you've chosen. Whether from the Bible or another ancient text, use this principle as a foundation to guide your journey. Keep this written vision somewhere visible, and let it serve as a reminder to stay aligned with your purpose.

4. **Take actionable steps in alignment with your guiding text**: Belief alone isn't enough; you must take practical steps toward your goal. Use your chosen text as motivation to act. For example, if you selected a scripture about faith and persistence, take a step that requires trust and determination. If you chose a teaching about generosity, find ways to give or support others while pursuing your own goals.

5. **Stay open to exploring different texts**: You are not limited to one tradition or text. Feel free to explore wisdom from various sources—be it spiritual, philosophical, or literary. By keeping an open mind and drawing from different wells of wisdom, you can find universal truths that resonate with your personal journey. Use these texts to guide your thoughts, actions, and decisions, trusting that ancient wisdom can offer relevant insights for modern challenges.

6. **Reflect on the results**: As you apply these principles and take action, reflect on the changes

in your life. How is this guiding text influencing your actions and your mindset? Are you seeing progress toward your desires? By regularly reviewing the wisdom you've chosen and adjusting your approach, you can ensure that you remain aligned with your deeper purpose.

8

Copy Others' Blueprint

This chapter delves into the importance of seeking out individuals who have achieved what you desire. It's not just about finding anyone who has achieved what you aspire to, but rather finding someone with whom you truly connect. Take the time to research this person and learn about their background, upbringing, and what led them to where they are today. Dive into interviews, books, and any other available resources to truly understand their journey. If this person offers courses, books, or seminars, I encourage you to take advantage of these opportunities. And if you know someone personally who has done what you desire to do, follow that person's blueprint if you know them to be credible. Take the time to understand who has mentored them and learn from them as well. Consider visiting the places that have been influential in their journey, such as their school or any institutions that have played a role in their success.

Take Notes

By immersing yourself in their world, you have the opportunity to learn from their experiences and gain valuable knowledge in a much shorter period of time. Embracing this approach could significantly accelerate your own path to success, potentially reducing the time it takes to achieve your goals from decades to just a few years or even less. It may require a high level of dedication and obsession, but the rewards will be worth it.

Studying the journeys of others is a crucial step in achieving your desires and establishing your vision.

My Experience with Studying Others

I realized how important it was to find others who were doing what I desired. I have always had a great passion for traveling. One of the major mistakes I made was not expressing to my relatives, whom I knew had traveled to different places, how important traveling was to me. Have you ever faced a similar challenge in pursuing your own desires?

I felt incredibly hurt when my family left me behind to babysit while others, especially relatives of my generation, went on a trip to Las Vegas. It felt like a missed opportunity. This mistake was very painful for me, and it prompted me to take notice of my peers. Two of my high school classmates posted photos of themselves studying abroad in different countries on social media. I was eager to leave the country. A few years later, during summer school at UCLA, my teacher's assistant was attentive and helpful in getting my peers, and I acclimated to the school as new transfer students. I could observe him closely because he was a teacher's aide in both of my classes.

One day, my teacher's assistant asked me, "Are you going to study abroad?" By then, I was so ready to graduate from school that I didn't want to add more time. I told him, "No". He immediately said to me with conviction, "You need to go study abroad!" Right after, he told me he did the study abroad program through another UC the summer before. "You can do that program." My teacher's assistant gave me all the information I needed: when the study abroad program applications were going to open up, where to find the office for study abroad, who the instructor was, and so on. As my teacher's assistant suggested, I decided to do that program because I didn't want to take extra time to search for a program. I trusted his suggestion. The following summer, I took my first overseas trip to Paris, France, and stayed for five weeks studying Jazz.

Mistake to Avoid: Not Asking for Help

In your journey, you may have encountered times when not speaking up about your desires or not seeking out guidance from others has slowed down your progress or caused unnecessary struggles. When I look back on my experience, I realize that by not expressing my deep desire to travel to those around me, I missed out on a family trip. I didn't let them know how much traveling meant to me, and because of that, I was left behind, feeling frustrated and disappointed.

Have you ever been in a situation where you wanted something but didn't share it with the right people? Or have you watched others achieving things you longed for and wished you had followed a similar path? When I didn't express my interest, I not only missed out on that family trip, but I also realized later how much faster I could have gotten to my own travel goals if I had paid closer attention to those who were already living the kind of experiences I wanted.

As I saw classmates studying abroad, I began to understand the value of observing and learning from those who were already achieving what I desired. By simply asking questions or seeking their guidance, I could have tapped into their wisdom sooner. When my teacher's assistant asked me if I was interested in studying abroad, his encouragement and detailed advice opened up an opportunity I might have otherwise missed. Because he had already taken the steps I wanted to take, I didn't have to waste time figuring out everything on my own. Instead, I followed his path and ended up experiencing the incredible opportunity to study abroad in Paris.

If we don't actively speak up about our interests to those who are already where we want to be, we risk missing out on guidance that can help us reach our desires faster. It's easy to think we have to figure it all out on our own, but that often leads to unnecessary hurdles or wasted time. By finding someone who is already doing what you want to do and learning from them—whether it's through a conversation, following their example, or even copying their blueprint—you can drastically shorten the time it takes to reach your goals.

When we don't ask for help or don't observe others who have already achieved what we want, we create longer, more difficult paths for ourselves. Whether it's because of pride, fear of rejection, or simply not realizing how valuable their experience can be, the result is often the same: frustration, delays, and missed opportunities.

By learning from others and copying their methods, you can avoid the common pitfalls and instead, move closer to your desires with much greater ease. Just like I trusted my teacher's assistant and followed his lead to study abroad, you can do the same with your goals. There's no shame in copying a proven path—in fact, it's one of the smartest ways to ensure you're on track to your desires.

Next Step

When setting your desires, seek credible individuals who achieve what you aspire to and follow the blueprint of the one you resonate with the most. Extract the steps they have taken, and if necessary, blend them with those of others who share similar lifestyles. Doing so can create your personal roadmap to your desired destination.

Here's a step to help you effectively learn from and model others who have already achieved what you desire:

1. **Identify role models who resonate with your goals**: Take time to research and find individuals who have successfully achieved what you aspire to—whether it's in your career, lifestyle, or personal growth. Choose people whose values, methods, and results align with your vision. Remember, the most effective role models aren't necessarily the most famous, but those whose journeys speak to where you want to go.

2. **Study their blueprint for success**: Once you've identified someone, delve deep into their journey. Look for interviews, articles, books, or even social media posts where they share insights about their path. Pay attention to the specific steps they took—whether it was acquiring new skills, adopting particular habits, or making key decisions at pivotal moments. Write down what stands out to you and consider how these steps apply to your own goals.

3. **Customize your plan**: While it's important to learn from others, remember that your journey is unique. Take the strategies that resonate the most with you and adjust them to fit your

specific circumstances, strengths, and aspirations. If multiple people inspire you, consider blending aspects of their journeys to create a custom roadmap that feels aligned with your personal vision and lifestyle.

4. **Take consistent action**: As you build your own roadmap from these blueprints, begin implementing the steps in your own life. Break down the actions you've learned into manageable goals, and commit to taking consistent steps toward them. Whether it's adopting a new habit, acquiring a skill, or seeking mentorship, small, consistent actions will build momentum toward your larger goals.

5. **Seek feedback and refine your approach**: Stay open to learning from both your successes and setbacks. As you implement your plan, don't hesitate to tweak your approach if something isn't working as you expected. The people you're modeling likely adjusted their own plans over time, so use flexibility and refinement as part of your process. Seek feedback from trusted sources or mentors, and make adjustments as needed.

6. **Maintain your authenticity**: While modeling others is a powerful strategy, it's equally important to stay true to your own voice, strengths, and desires. Use the blueprint of others as a guide, but avoid feeling the pressure to copy their every move. As you progress, you'll begin to discover your unique way of achieving success that reflects who you truly are.

9

Know When to Pivot

Why Pivot

When it comes to achieving our goals and desires, knowing when to pivot is crucial. Sometimes, the path we are on may not be the right one at the moment, and going in a different direction is necessary. It may require taking a new step, adding or eliminating a step, or even setting aside the desire for a period of time. If obstacles are coming against us, it's a good opportunity to approach our goal from a different angle. We may need to look at it from a different perspective or focus on something else for a while. Giving our desires some breathing room or pursuing a different desire altogether can also be beneficial.

Being open to different possibilities and not being afraid of making pivots are important. There are countless desires to choose from, and sometimes, pursuing a completely different desire or letting one desire lead to another can lead to greater fulfillment. So, for pivoting, don't be afraid to make the move that could lead to attaining what you truly desire.

I have a natural talent for recognizing when to pivot and carrying out the action. Pivoting is a subtle step that many people either don't know how to take or fear taking because they worry they won't be able to return to their original goal or fear being seen as giving up. However, recognizing when to pivot is a valuable method to help us attain our goals.

Why I Needed to Pivot

Have you ever faced a challenge where you felt that your current approach to achieving your goal just wasn't working? I've been there, too. I encountered this challenge during my first two years of community college when I wasn't sure how to attend a four-year university while majoring in film studies. It seemed like reaching my goal was becoming increasingly unrealistic. So, I decided to take six months off from community college, which was a significant pivot for me as it was the longest break I had taken from school up to that point. During that time, I discovered that film institutions were available for me to attend. By the end of my six-month break, I applied and was accepted into an 18-month film program I completed in 13 months.

When I Made a Pivot

During my fourth month in this program, I decided that I wanted to attend UCLA. That's when I realized I needed to go back to community college to finish my general education courses before transferring to UCLA. Upon finishing the film program, I took up film projects, and within four months of graduating from film school, I returned to community college to continue my general education journey. Initially, I planned to give myself two years to finish community college before transferring, but after consulting with a counselor, I found out I only needed one year. So, I applied that fall and was accepted the following spring, with plans to start at UCLA the next academic year.

Through knowing when to pivot and embracing the idea that a different move can still lead to my desired goal, even if it's not directly aligned with my initial plans, I was able to explore other paths that ultimately led me to my goal of attending UCLA. Pivoting allowed me to experience avenues that I hadn't considered before, and it enabled me to attend an all-film school institution and another community college that helped me transfer to UCLA.

In the past, people rarely discussed the concept of pivoting. It was typically believed that there was only one way to achieve something, with little consideration for alternative approaches. This rigidity sometimes hinders individuals from pursuing their genuine desires when presented with obstacles. Nowadays, people are more open to considering different routes to reach their goals.

One common mistake is either not recognizing the need to pivot or being afraid to pivot and explore new avenues.

Mistake to Avoid: Fear of Pivoting

If you don't know when to pivot, it can lead to unnecessary challenges, frustration, and even the desire to give up on your goal entirely. In my own experience, when I first set out to major in film studies at a four-year university, I hit a wall. It felt like no matter what I tried, I just couldn't figure out how to make it work. If I had stayed stuck on that initial approach, I might still be struggling to find my way. But by taking a step back and pivoting—choosing to take a break, reassess, and then explore other options like attending a film school first— I was able to make progress in a new direction. This eventually led me back to my original goal of attending UCLA, just by a different route.

For you, it might feel like the goal you're pursuing has hit a standstill, or maybe the path you're on isn't as clear as you hoped. When that happens, it's tempting to stay the course out of fear of change or because you believe there's only one right way to achieve what you want. However, continuing down a path that isn't working can not only slow your progress but also drain your energy and motivation. You may find yourself feeling stuck, questioning your abilities, and wondering if your goal is even attainable.

The truth is, knowing when to pivot is essential for long-term success. Pivoting doesn't mean giving up on your dreams—it means being adaptable enough to explore other paths that may lead you there in a different, often better, way. Just like in my case, I had to realize that the film studies goal wasn't dead, but it required a different approach. By staying flexible and willing to shift gears when necessary, you open yourself up to new opportunities that might be even more aligned with what you really want.

If you don't recognize the need to pivot, you may also risk missing out on valuable experiences and opportunities. The frustration of hitting roadblocks can cause you to doubt your dreams, and the longer you hold on to a plan that isn't working, the more discouraged you may feel. However, when you learn to recognize when it's time to adjust your approach, you create space for new solutions and directions to appear.

It's important to understand that pivoting is not failure—it's a strategy for success. It's about being proactive and not waiting for circumstances to force you into a corner. The willingness to pivot can save you time and energy while ultimately helping you achieve your desires in a more fulfilling and effective way. By adapting your strategy when needed, you can avoid the frustration of feeling like you're spinning your wheels, and instead, get closer to your goals with renewed momentum.

Next Step

Being open-minded to the possibility of alternative paths and realizing that if something is truly meant for you, you will find your way back to it, even after taking multiple pivots or making major changes to your path, is key to successful pivoting. Open up to the idea that there may be another avenue for you to achieve your desired goal. If it's truly meant for you, you can attain it regardless of the number of pivots along the way.

Here's a step to help you navigate pivoting with purpose while staying aligned with your ultimate goal:

1. **Assess your current path**: Take time to reflect on where you are right now in your journey. Is the path you're on still aligned with your desired outcome, or are there obstacles that seem immovable? Sometimes, the signs that it's time to pivot include persistent roadblocks, lack of fulfillment, or the sense that the current approach isn't bringing you closer to your goal. Being honest with yourself about your progress is the first step in knowing when to pivot.

2. **Identify alternative paths**: Once you've assessed your current situation, start exploring other potential ways to reach your goal. This could mean changing your strategy, seeking new opportunities, or even shifting to a related goal that may be more aligned with your current skills

or circumstances. Write down a few alternative paths you could take, and consider how they might offer fresh perspectives or open new doors to success.

3. **Trust the process**: Understand that pivots are a natural part of the journey. Just because you're taking a new route doesn't mean you've failed—it's simply a redirection. Remind yourself that if your goal is truly meant for you, the new path could be the one that leads you there. Trust that every pivot provides new opportunities for growth and learning, even if it feels uncomfortable at first.

4. **Take small, intentional steps**: Rather than making drastic changes all at once, start by making smaller, intentional shifts in your approach. Test out new strategies or explore alternative routes while still keeping your end goal in sight. These small pivots allow you to experiment without feeling overwhelmed by a complete overhaul.

5. **Stay flexible and open-minded**: As you pivot, remain flexible and open to what unfolds. There may be unexpected detours that bring you closer to your goal in ways you hadn't imagined. Be willing to adapt, adjust, and rethink your plan if needed. Staying flexible helps you navigate the challenges that arise without feeling discouraged or stuck.

6. **Celebrate progress, not perfection**: As you pivot and explore new paths, celebrate your progress rather than focusing solely on the outcome. Every pivot, whether small or large, is a step toward your goal. Recognize the growth and learning that come from each adjustment, and trust that with persistence and patience, you'll reach your destination—even if the path looks different from what you originally envisioned.

PART 3 - HAVE

Cultivate gratitude and appreciation, establish a due date, and understand your W.H.Y. To 'HAVE' means "to own, possess, be subject to, and experience."

10

W.H.Y.

Your W.H.Y.

Understanding the reason behind your desire is imperative in reaching your goal. Your WHY is critical - it drives you to take the necessary steps. An acronym for "why" is "what hurts you." Often, our past pains are the driving force behind our goals. This ties back to an earlier chapter in the book where we discussed finding solutions to problems, sometimes stemming from negative past experiences. Your "why" can catalyze the change you want to see in your life, propelling you toward your goal. Once you uncover your why, the other steps to reaching your goal will become clear. Finding your purpose is critical.

My W.H.Y. Experience

When I first considered attending college, my purpose was not strong enough. As a result, I neither received acceptance or rejection letters. I did not want to be left out of conversations among my peers about colleges. This desire, coupled with the pressure from teachers to pursue higher education, led me to lack a strong purpose. I was not committed, and this was why I did not get accepted to any colleges. Eventually, I acknowledged that I still wanted to go to school and would figure out a stronger "why" later. My purpose was strong enough for me to start at a community college and then transition to a four-year institution.

Have you ever struggled to define your purpose? It took me years to realize that I aimed to help individuals interested in college. After attending five different colleges, my strong purpose emerged from my experiences and struggles. My purpose evolved from wanting to be part of conversations to wanting to support others on their college journey. I care about encouraging individuals to be specific about their goals and aspirations when going to college.

Define Your Purpose

In defining your purpose, one of the most powerful places to start is by understanding what deeply affects you—what hurts you. Often, the source of your purpose lies within your pain, struggles, or frustrations, either from your own experiences or those you've witnessed around you. Perhaps it's a challenge you've personally faced, a problem you've observed in your community, or a troubling situation from your past that continues to weigh on your heart. By reflecting on what stirs you emotionally, you can identify what truly matters to you. This awareness is crucial because it gives your vision depth and authenticity.

The most common mistake people make when pursuing their vision is not having a strong enough "why." Without a compelling reason that pulls you forward, it's easy to lose motivation when obstacles arise. But when your "why" is rooted in something that truly moves you, especially when it's connected to helping others, it becomes more than just a goal—it becomes a mission. A purpose centered around making a difference for others has an incredible power to sustain you, even during the most difficult times.

When your vision extends beyond personal gain and aligns with the idea of serving a greater good, your passion naturally grows stronger. Your "why" becomes a source of inspiration not only for yourself but also for those around you. A purpose-driven life gives your vision the fuel it needs to become a reality. Your desire and vision, when tied to a higher purpose, become forces of change, motivating you to persevere regardless of the challenges you face.

Mistake to Avoid: Not Having a Compelling WHY

When you don't have a compelling WHY—when you haven't clearly identified "What Hurts You"—you run the risk of losing momentum or even feeling inadequate in your pursuit of a desire or vision. Without that deep-rooted purpose driving you forward, the challenges you inevitably face can seem overwhelming, and your goals might start to feel unattainable. Have you ever felt like giving up because things became too hard or the obstacles seemed too great? If so, it's possible that your purpose—your "why"—wasn't fully defined.

I experienced this firsthand when I first considered attending college. At the time, my purpose for going to college was not strong enough, which led to me feeling uncertain and uncommitted. I applied to several schools, but I neither received acceptance nor rejection letters. I realized that the lack of a strong purpose left me floating in limbo. My initial desire to attend college stemmed more from wanting to be part of the conversations my peers were having about higher education, and from the pressure of teachers encouraging us to go to college, than from a true personal drive. This lack of clarity about why I wanted to go left me feeling lost, and I didn't make it into any of the schools I applied to.

Eventually, I acknowledged that I still wanted to attend college, but I knew I had to figure out a stronger "why"—a deeper purpose that would sustain me. That realization led me to community college, and over time, my purpose evolved. Through my experiences and struggles, I discovered that my true passion was helping others navigate the college journey. What started as a weak reason for going to college transformed into a meaningful purpose: to encourage others to define their goals and aspirations more clearly. By understanding what hurt me—my struggles with college applications and direction—I found my purpose.

If you don't take the time to figure out your "why," you may end up pursuing a goal that doesn't align with your true passions or one that lacks the emotional weight needed to keep you going. This disconnect can lead to frustration, burnout, or even giving up altogether. But when you identify the core reason behind your desire— especially if it's rooted in something that has caused you pain or something you deeply care about—you'll find the strength and resilience to keep moving forward, even when the journey becomes difficult.

So, take the time to reflect on your own "What Hurts You." Is there something that stirs you to act? Maybe it's a personal challenge you've faced or an injustice you've seen in the world that you want to change. Whatever it is, make sure your purpose is connected to something that matters deeply to you. When your purpose is clear, it doesn't just give you a reason to chase your vision; it gives you the motivation and grit to overcome any obstacle that stands in your way. Your purpose becomes the fire that keeps your desire alive, no matter how hard the road gets.

Next Step

Once you find your purpose, you gain the confidence to pursue your goals and desires. It is the driving force behind your commitment and determination. So, remember to start with what hurts you, something you are passionate about solving or improving. You will find the passion and confidence to attain your desires when you identify your purpose.

Here's a step to help you connect with your "WHY" and use it to fuel your vision:

1. **Reflect on what truly moves you**: Take a moment to think about the challenges, injustices, or issues in the world that deeply affect you. What breaks your heart? What lights a fire within you to take action? These are often clues that lead you to your purpose. Write down the first thoughts or feelings that come to mind when you reflect on what you're passionate about changing or improving.

2. **Identify your personal connection**: Consider why this issue matters to you on a personal level. It could be connected to your own experiences, the people you care about, or the future you want to create. Understanding the emotional connection to your "WHY" will deepen your sense of purpose and give you a stronger foundation to pursue your vision.

3. **Define your "WHY" clearly**: Once you've identified the issue that drives you, articulate your "WHY" in a clear, concise statement. For example, "I am passionate about empowering young people to achieve their potential because

I know firsthand the impact of mentorship" or "I want to create a business that helps people reduce waste because I care about protecting our planet for future generations." This clarity will keep you focused and motivated when challenges arise.

4. **Align your goals with your "WHY"**: Now, think about how your goals align with your purpose. Your "WHY" should be the foundation for all the goals and desires you set, ensuring they reflect your larger mission. Take a look at your current goals and adjust them if necessary to make sure they are connected to your deeper "WHY."

5. **Use your "WHY" as a motivator**: Whenever you face setbacks or doubt, revisit your "WHY." Let it remind you of the greater purpose behind your vision. Visualize the positive change you'll create, not just for yourself but for others, and let that energize you to keep moving forward, even when things get tough.

6. **Stay committed and revisit often**: As you grow and evolve, your "WHY" may shift slightly, or you may uncover new layers of purpose. Make it a habit to revisit your "WHY" regularly, reflect on its significance, and adjust your goals accordingly. Staying connected to your purpose will keep you aligned with your true vision.

11

Due Date

Set Your Due Date

Setting a due date for your goal serves as a way to give yourself a clear timeline for accomplishing it. This due date shows that you have purpose and intention behind your actions and forces you to be attentive and intentional in your pursuit. It's akin to having a due date for writing a paper - you know exactly how much time you have to research, write, and submit it. This due date makes your desire more realistic and gives you a greater reason to work towards achieving it. Without a due date, losing motivation or not taking your goal seriously is easy. It provides the accountability and drive you need to stay focused and achieve your desired goals.

Stick with Due Date

It's important to stick to the due date for your goal as much as possible. Frequent changes can lead to doubt or uncertainty about achieving it. Choose a date and commit to it to show your determination. However, it's okay to adjust the date if necessary. For example, if you planned to finish community college in two years but faced unexpected challenges, it's acceptable to extend the timeline. Just make sure there is a significant reason for doing so to ensure you reach your goal effectively.

Importance of Due Date

Determining the due date for your desired goal strengthens your commitment to achieving your desire. Having a due date can be challenging, but not having one is even more so, as it is easy to lose focus without one. Personally, I find it difficult to remain on track toward my goals when there is no specified due date. Have you encountered challenges related to establishing or adhering to a due date for your goals? For me, having one significantly aids in maintaining focus. Knowing that there is a set date keeps me accountable and motivated to achieve my goal.

My Due Date Experience

An example of the power of setting a due date is when my partner and I made the decision to move out of his relative's home. Rather than just talking about it or hoping that it would happen eventually, we took a concrete step—we set a specific date for our move. This date became more than just a deadline; it became a target, a constant reminder of our shared goal and the commitment we made to each other. Having this due date gave us a sense of urgency and accountability, ensuring that our desire to relocate stayed front and center in our minds.

On the decided date, we successfully relocated, and because we had a clear target in mind, we were able to take care of all the necessary arrangements well in advance. We informed family members, scouted potential places to live, and secured a place that met our needs. That date on the calendar gave us the sense of urgency we needed to push forward, even when challenges came up.

In the end, the due date not only helped us stay focused, but it also showed others that we were serious about our goal. It demonstrated our commitment and created momentum, allowing us to tackle obstacles with determination and drive. Without the due date, we could have easily delayed our plans or let distractions steer us off course. But with that target in place, we had no choice but to confront challenges head-on, making it clear that we were dedicated to achieving our goal. Setting a deadline transformed our intention into action and gave us the push we needed to make it happen.

Mistake to Avoid: Neglecting Setting a Due Date

If you don't have a due date for your goal or vision, it becomes easy to lose focus and stay uncommitted, which often leads to the vision falling by the wayside. When we leave things open-ended without a clear target, it creates room for distractions, excuses, and hesitation. Without a set timeline, the sense of urgency that drives progress diminishes, and what could have been a well-executed plan turns into wishful thinking.

In my own experience, setting a due date was the key to making my goal of relocating a reality. Without it, my partner and I might have continued discussing the move indefinitely, letting everyday life take over and push our plans further down the line. But by setting that specific date, we created a tangible deadline—a point in time that kept us accountable. We knew exactly when we needed to act, and it pushed us to organize every step of the process ahead of time.

Imagine if we hadn't set that date. We might have put off conversations with family members, delayed searching for places to live, or hesitated to make any real decisions until we "felt ready." This could have gone on for months or even years, with the move constantly feeling like something we would eventually get around to. But with a due date, there was no "someday." There was only that specific target, and each day leading up to it became focused on preparing for the move.

For you, it might be a different goal, but the principle remains the same. Whether it's completing a project, achieving a personal milestone, or realizing a vision, not having a deadline creates room for procrastination and uncertainty. When there's no sense of urgency, it's easy to allow your goal to slip to the bottom of your priority list. You might think, "I'll get to it eventually," but without a due date, that "eventually" could stretch on indefinitely.

Without a clear target, you may also struggle with commitment. When there's no end point in sight, it's difficult to maintain the focus and energy needed to push through challenges. Obstacles can feel like reasons to delay or give up entirely because there's no pressing need to overcome them in a timely manner. But when you have a firm deadline, there's less room for hesitation. You're forced to address challenges head-on because the clock is ticking, and every moment counts toward achieving your goal.

Setting a due date isn't just about having a deadline—it's about creating momentum. It's a tool that helps you stay committed, remain accountable, and act with purpose. Without it, you run the risk of losing your way and letting your vision slip further from reach. But when you set a date, you're declaring that your goal is not just a possibility, but a priority. You give yourself a reason to stay focused, take action, and ultimately fulfill your vision.

Next Step

A common mistake people make in pursuing their goals is failing to establish an end date. Setting a realistic date and informing individuals who can hold you accountable or assist you in achieving it is crucial. This adds external accountability and demonstrates your seriousness about your goal to those around you. Through careful planning and accountability, attaining the desired end date is achievable.

Here's a step to help you set a due date and stay committed to achieving your vision:

1. **Set a clear, realistic deadline**: Begin by identifying a specific, measurable goal you want to achieve and set a due date that challenges you but remains realistic. Consider the complexity of your vision and how much time you can dedicate to it daily or weekly. Write this deadline down and place it somewhere visible—on your calendar, phone, or a place where you'll see it often as a constant reminder.

2. **Break your goal into smaller milestones**: A long-term goal can feel overwhelming, so break it down into smaller, manageable steps. Create mini-deadlines for each milestone that build toward your larger goal. These smaller victories will help you stay motivated and on track. Use your due date as a marker for achieving each milestone, creating a clear path forward.

3. **Communicate your due date to an accountability partner**: Choose someone you trust—whether a friend, mentor, or colleague—who will check in with you regularly. Share your due date with them and ask for their support in

holding you accountable. Having someone to answer to can provide that extra push when motivation wanes and help keep you on course.

4. **Develop a schedule and routine**: Create a structured plan to work toward your vision daily or weekly. A consistent routine helps maintain progress and reinforces discipline. Schedule specific time blocks dedicated to taking action on your goals. Stick to your routine as closely as possible, even if some days you make small progress—it's the accumulation of consistent effort that brings results.

5. **Track your progress and adjust as needed**: Monitor your progress regularly to ensure you're moving toward your due date. If unforeseen challenges arise, don't hesitate to adjust your schedule or extend your deadline. Flexibility is important, but be careful not to let this turn into procrastination. Keep the focus on progress, not perfection.

6. **Celebrate your achievements along the way**: As you reach each milestone, celebrate your wins. Recognizing your achievements, no matter how small, can help you stay positive and motivated. Use these moments to build momentum and remind yourself how much closer you are to your ultimate vision.

12

Gratitude and Appreciation

Since many of us use Gratitude and appreciation interchangeably, I will be expressing how both are fundamental pillars of manifestation. It requires being thankful and estimating the quality and worth of something for what we already have and believing we will receive what we desire. Expressing gratitude /appreciation has a powerful effect on our bodies; it neutralizes negativity and elevates our vibrations. Cultivating a grateful/appreciative mindset deflects anything that does not align with our desires. It opens us up to new possibilities and higher vibrations. By acknowledging what we're grateful for and appreciating what we already have, we can see that with the right mindset, we can achieve our true desires.

Difference between Gratitude and Appreciation

The etymology of 'Gratitude' mid-1500 "goodwill," from Latin *gratus,* means "thankfulness, pleasing." PIE root 'gwere' "to favor".

The etymology of 'Appreciation' circa 1600 "act if estimating the quality and worth of something," from Late Latin *appretiare* meaning "estimate the quality of". 'Appreciate' 1650s, "to estimate or value highly" from Late Latin *appretiare* {break the word down} from *ad* which means "to" + *pretium* which mean "price".

Your Brain on Gratitude

Expressing gratitude daily can rewire the brain through the process of neuroplasticity, which is the brain's ability to form and reorganize synaptic connections, especially in response to learning or experience. When you consistently practice gratitude, your brain begins to create new neural pathways that are specifically associated with feelings of appreciation and positivity. Each time you focus on gratitude, those pathways are activated and reinforced, making it easier and more natural for you to access feelings of thankfulness in the future.

Over time, this practice leads to a shift in the brain's default mode—where it naturally starts to focus more on the positive aspects of life rather than dwelling on negativity. As a result, not only does your mindset become more positive, but you also start to experience greater emotional resilience, improved mental well-being, and an overall sense of happiness. Your brain essentially "adapts" to this new pattern of thinking, making gratitude a powerful tool for fostering long-term positivity and emotional health.

My Experience with Gratitude and Appreciation

Gratitude/appreciation is a simple acknowledgment of the good that's happened or is happening in your life. My mistake was not expressing gratitude/appreciation and focusing on what I did not have. Have you experienced this before?

My lack of gratitude/appreciation only lengthened the journey towards my desires. It even caused me to forget what I was truly aiming for. For instance, while living at my boyfriend's relative's home, I struggled to be grateful/appreciative for the situation. It took me time to realize that my lack of gratitude/appreciation kept me stuck. When I shifted my perspective and began expressing gratitude/appreciation for my circumstances, I slowly started to see how I could assist in my living space. Helping out around the house granted me a bit more grace from my boyfriend's relatives to stay longer in their home while I got my life together. I recognized that being grateful/appreciative opened me up to new possibilities and attracted the support I needed.

Mistake to Avoid: Lacking Gratitude and Appreciation

If we don't practice gratitude and appreciation, it's easy to lose sight of the blessings already present in our lives. A lack of gratitude and appreciation creates a mindset where we are always chasing after what we don't have, feeling as though something is missing. In doing so, we not only overlook the resources, relationships, and opportunities right in front of us, but we also rob ourselves of the joy and contentment that comes with acknowledging what's good in our current situation.

In my experience, when I struggled to express gratitude for my living situation at my boyfriend's relative's home, I felt stuck and dissatisfied. Instead of appreciating the shelter and support I was receiving, I focused on what I didn't have—my own place, more freedom, or a different living environment. This lack of gratitude clouded my ability to see the good that was right in front of me and made the situation feel more difficult than it actually was.

The moment I shifted my perspective and began to express genuine gratitude for the roof over my head, the help I was receiving, and the opportunity to get back on my feet, everything started to change. I realized that by appreciating the space I was in and the people who were helping me, I was able to open myself up to new ways of contributing to the household and fostering positive relationships. That shift in gratitude allowed me to see the support I had rather than focusing on what I was missing. It also showed others that I was willing to pitch in and help, which made the living situation much more harmonious.

For many people, the mistake is thinking that we will be grateful only once we achieve our goals or get what we desire. But in reality, practicing gratitude right now can create the space for more opportunities, support, and positive experiences to come into our lives. When we don't show appreciation for what we already have, it's easy to fall into a mindset of lack, always searching for something outside of ourselves to fill the void.

By neglecting gratitude, we risk living in a state of dissatisfaction, unable to appreciate what's already working in our favor. This can make the journey to achieving our desires feel longer and more challenging, because we aren't fully grounded in the present moment. When we express gratitude, we remind ourselves of our blessings, stay connected to what's important, and invite more abundance into our lives. Gratitude can turn what we already have into enough, and from that place of contentment, we can attract even more of what we desire.

Next Step

My suggestion to the reader is to refrain from complaining about what you lack and focus on expressing gratitude/appreciation for what you do have, no matter how small. This simple shift in mindset can reveal the abundance already present and align us with the people and opportunities that can help us achieve our desires. Stop complaining and speak genuinely about the things and people for whom you are grateful/appreciative. Doing so allows you to open yourselves up to the solutions and support you need to bring your vision to life.

Here's a step to help you practice gratitude and appreciation daily:

1. **Start a gratitude journal**: Each day, write down three to five things you are genuinely grateful for, whether big or small. It could be a supportive conversation, a small success, or even something as simple as a warm cup of coffee. By doing this regularly, you'll begin to notice how much you have to appreciate in your life. This daily practice will shift your focus from what you lack to what you already possess.

2. **Shift your thoughts from complaints to appreciation**: The next time you catch yourself about to complain about something, stop for a moment and reframe the situation. Ask yourself: "What is there to appreciate here?" For example, instead of complaining about a difficult task, express appreciation for the opportunity to grow and improve your skills. This shift in perspective can change your entire mood and outlook.

3. **Express gratitude to others regularly**: Make it a habit to tell the people in your life that you appreciate them. This could be through a quick

text, a note, or a heartfelt conversation. Acknowledging others' efforts and support not only strengthens your relationships but also helps you become more attuned to the positive energy around you.

4. **Visualize abundance in your life**: After writing in your gratitude journal or taking a moment to appreciate what you have, close your eyes and visualize your life as abundant, full of possibilities, and aligned with your desires. Feel grateful for the opportunities yet to come, and trust that your gratitude is attracting more of what you want into your life.

5. **Turn challenges into opportunities for growth**: When faced with obstacles, rather than focusing on the negative, ask yourself, "What can I learn from this?" or "How can this challenge make me stronger?" Shifting from frustration to gratitude in difficult moments will help you see that every experience brings value.

6. **Commit to daily gratitude practice**: For at least the next 30 days, commit to practicing gratitude daily. Whether it's through journaling, thanking someone, or simply reflecting on what you appreciate, the consistency will build a mindset of abundance and positivity that will naturally align you with solutions and opportunities for growth.

TO THE READER

This book is a roadmap to help you achieve the results you seek. Embrace your vision every day. Your imagination is a powerful tool, so don't be afraid to use it! Remember that everything you use in your daily life, from your bed to the space shuttle, originated from someone's imagination. Be deliberate in your thoughts, words, and actions, and practice, drill, and rehearse the life you want to create. Focus on yourself first before trying to help others. Once you become adept at achieving your goals, your success will be evident to others, and they will be curious about your methods. Then, you can share your wisdom with confidence. Remember, you are in control.

MY APPRECIATION

I appreciate you, my husband, Brandon, for manifesting me in your life.

I appreciate you, my son, Maxwell, for choosing me to be the vessel you came through and fulfilling my manifestation.

I appreciate you both, my mother, Mia, and you, my father, Enrique, for creating your best and only collaborative manifestation, ME! I appreciate you both as artists. From each of you I gained love and skills, genetically, in multiple art forms. I appreciate you, momma, for supporting me in my artistic expressions throughout my life. I appreciate you, father, for being an attentive listener these past few years and supporting me in this book journey.

I appreciate you, my granny, Charlotte, who has been my number 1 cheerleader and immense supporter since I was born, especially throughout my artistry. I appreciate you and view you as my first art instructor in multiple art forms. Much gratitude for pushing me to practice in elementary which carried on until my present.

I appreciate my grandpa, Eldred (Rest in Peace), for keeping me close to him for the first 7 years of my life and giving me the freedom that no one else gave me at such an early age.

I appreciate you, my aunt, Lesley, for allowing me to live with you and my cousins for 5 years (11 to 16 years old). It was during these years that I became intentional with my imagination. I appreciate you, my cousins/siblings, Thomas, BiJon and Jeremiah for those years of co-creating with me.

I appreciate you, my uncles, Jai and Cleveland for expanding my mind in the technical and mechanical fields that allowed me to articulate myself creatively in multiple art forms.

I appreciate you, my younger brother, Christopher, for supporting and cheering me on in anything I do.

I appreciate you, my Nana, Helen, for supporting me in my life as your own. I appreciate you, Aunt Kassie, for helping me tap into faculties of mind as a teenager.

I appreciate my aunt, Marcia (Rest in Peace), for paving the way for authorship.

I appreciate you, my aunt, Sonia, for encouraging me to be myself, unapologetically.

I appreciate you, my aunt, Rochelle, for cheering me on, supporting me and your highly encouraging words for my new venture of authorship.

I appreciate you, my brother from another mother, Roosevelt, for supporting me since 9th grade with just about every project I either came up with or was involved in, including my authorship.

I appreciate you, my siblings, my aunts & uncles, my cousins, my Godson & Goddaughters and my step-dad for working with me through my continuous creative development.

I appreciate you, The Barlow Sisters, for many decades of connecting and creativity.

I appreciate you, my high school best friends & peers, my praise dance sisters, my film school peers and my poetry peers at my university for challenging me creatively and imaginatively.

I appreciate you, my mentor/godmom, Kristin, for supporting my artistry and introducing me to knowledge and places in support of my artistry.

I appreciate you, my bonus dad, Robert, for supporting me with enthusiasm.

I appreciate you, my bonus mom, Melissa, for supporting me with care.

I appreciate you, ***my Elementary School***: my kindergarten instructors: Ms. Pitts, Mrs. Henderson, my 3rd grade instructor, Mrs. McClaren, my 3rd, 4th & 5th grade instructor, Mrs. Price, my American Sign Language and Spanish instructor, Mrs. J. Brooks, my after school Booster Club program instructors, Ms. S. Sims & Ms. Douglas, my after school instructors: Mr. Blessingame, Mrs. Carter, my Choir director, Dr. Alexander; ***my Middle School***: my 6th grade Honors English & History/Acting instructor Ms. Muhammad; my 6th grade

Basketball coach, Monika; my Personal Guitar Lessons instructor, Mr. Martin; my 7th grade Leadership instructor, Ms. Donerson, my 8th grade History instructor, Mr. Pierre; *my High School*: my 9th grade Music Tech instructor and Music Magnet coordinator Mr. Jackson, my 9th grade Honors English instructor, Ms. Beatty, my 10th grade Theater instructor, Ms. Fox, my Music Magnet counselor, Mr. Harris (Rest in Peace), my 11th grade English Literature instructor, Mrs. Harrison-Owens, my 12th grade English instructor, Mrs. DeJaun, my 11th/12th grade Film Academy instructors, Mr. McCane and Mr. Owens, my Band instructors Mr. Hogan, Mr. Crawford, & Mr. Martinez, my Choir instructor, Mr. Hines, and my Dance instructor Mrs. Tell Coffield, Thelonius Monk Institute's Bebop to Hip Hop Program director, Daniel Seeff; *Churches*: my Spiritual Leaders, Pastor Taylor, Pastor Bob & Mrs. Pat, Pastor & Sister Crutcher, Sister Parker, Apostle Pauline, Pastor & First Lady Hines, my Praise Dance team instructors, Dr. Kristal, Ms. Sharon, & Ms. Bridgette, my Young Adult Sunday School instructor, Ansonia, my Junior Choir director, Pastor Lisa, my Young Adult Ministry instructor, Mrs. Kishaa, and my Praise Dance team manager, Rhandi; *my Community Colleges*: my English 101 instructor, Professor Norwood, my African American Studies instructor, Professor H. Ealy & Dr. Eckhart; *my University school*: my Peer Learning Facilitator, Terrence, my Spoken Word instructor, Professor B. Bain; *my Film School*: my Senior

Admissions Rep, Reason, my Boom Operating instructor, Mr. J. Coburn IV, my Film Editor instructor, Mr. M. Heselov, my Sound Design instructor, ; *my University school campus Theater (House Management) job*: my supervisors, Ron, Ernesto, Pia, Duong, Melhi, James, Cory, Randy, and Gena; and *my schooling*: my Instructors, Soke Johnny Revels Sr. and Sundon Shahid, for introducing me to knowledge that has expanded my mind, enriched, evoked and challenged my creativity and imagination in life, art and leadership.

I appreciate you, The Shorters, The Neals, The LeBlancs, and Mr. Mullen (Rest in Peace), for adopting me into your tribes & homes when I was a young one and giving me blueprints to imagine having homeownership.

I appreciate you, my Mother-in-Love, Avis, for being open-minded and willing to touch and agree with the vision me, Brandon and Maxwell share with you.

I appreciate you, Mr. & Mrs. Walker for allowing me to live in your home where I started my journey of Enlightenment.

I appreciate you, DJ Sayso, Onyekachi Kenis, and Roderick Talley, for encouraging me in this authorship field in my peer group.

I appreciate you, Ms. Lauryn Hill, and your team for your album *The Miseducation of Lauryn Hill*. This album literally changed my life.

I appreciate you, artists: Kirk Franklin, B.o.B, Jerry LaVigne Jr, Tank and the Bangas, Daylyt, and Durand Bernarr for sharing your art. You all artistries helped me maneuver in this world and showed me in many ways how to be even more open with my artistry.

I appreciate Bobby Hemmitt and Brother Panic (Rest in Peace), who were the first people I came across to emphasize the importance of the human imagination and "doing the work" in using the imagination.

I appreciate The Imagination Guru Ministries and Abundance Community Network. Joining these two communities has enriched me and my household.

I appreciate you, my editor early in this process of this book, Maryam Nawaz, for ensuring that my book reads smoothly and correcting all my errors.

I appreciate you, Muhammad Nadeem, for making certain that my book looked appropriate and giving quality work.

I appreciate all who are reading this book. Please share this with others, especially when you get the results you have been seeking.

ABOUT THE AUTHOR

Alexandria Patterson was born and raised in South Central Los Angeles to a Californian mother and a Costa Rican father. She was primarily raised by her mother's family and her younger brother's father's family, with limited contact with her father from ages 7 to 12. As a result, Alexandria had little knowledge of her Costa Rican heritage.

Growing up, Alexandria turned to various art forms to fill the void left by her father's absence, using her imagination to create the environments she longed for. During her junior year in high school, she discovered a passion for filmmaking. In her senior year, she received three Video in the Classroom Awards for the Los Angeles Unified School District for her high school PSA short film televised on KLCS (an instructional television station for LAUSD) in Los Angeles.

Alexandria moved to Nevada with her partner after studying at The Los Angeles Film School and the University of California, Los Angeles.

Nevada is where she reconnected with her father and paternal family for the first time in almost two decades.

Alexandria graduated from The Los Angeles Film School with her Associate Degree in Film/Cinema and a Bachelor's Degree in African-American Studies from the University of California, Los Angeles.

She now lives with her partner and their son, continuing to imagine their best lives and enjoy gratifying experiences together.